TRIED BUT UNTESTED

The aims and outcomes of
sex education in schools

TRIED BUT UNTESTED

The aims and outcomes of
sex education in schools

Edited by Paul Danon

FAMILY EDUCATION TRUST

TRIED BUT UNTESTED

The aims and outcomes of
sex education in schools

published for

FAMILY EDUCATION TRUST

by

FAMILY PUBLICATIONS

77 BANBURY ROAD, OXFORD, OX2 6LF

Tel: 01865 514408   *Fax:* 01865 52774

ISBN 0 906229 12 X

Printed in England by BPC Wheatons Ltd, Exeter

"Men who begin by boasting that they have cast away all dogmas go on to be incessantly, imprudently, and quite irrationally dogmatic . . . It is all the worse because the dogmas are generally concerned with very delicate human relations . . . these dogmas always directly attack fathers and wives and children, without offering either credentials or evidence. The general rule is that nothing must be accepted on any ancient or admitted authority, but everything must be accepted on any new or nameless authority or accepted even more eagerly on no authority at all."

All is Grist
G K Chesterton, New York, 1932

Contents

Contents

Introduction

Baroness Elles

Over the last three decades powerful lobbies and pressure groups have campaigned for sex education in schools. As a consequence, teachers are giving their pupils material and information which, forty years ago, would have been considered obscene or pornographic. Children to whom such material was shown would have been judged in need of care and protection.

Although the main direction of sex education has remained the same, the emphasis has changed over the decades. In the early 1960s, sex education concentrated on the theme of population and the supposed lack of resources to meet the needs of more and more births. It was asserted that contraceptive advice was required for all women of child-bearing age, as well as for young people about to enter that age range. It was not considered relevant that among the most pressing of problems for western Europe was actually the disposal of surplus food. Nor was it thought significant that the decline in the number of live births in western Europe was already adversely affecting the demographic balance between the young and the old.

In the 1970s the accent was placed on unwanted pregnancy. Contraceptive advice began to be given on a wider scale to girls well below the legal age of consent, though the number of teenage pregnancies nevertheless increased.

The 1980s witnessed an increasing number of abortions and, although the government's aim – stated in its *Health of the Nation* document – has been to reduce that number, Britain came to have the highest number of teenage pregnancies in Europe. In 1981, 45 out of every 1000 girls between 15 and 19 became pregnant outside marriage. Now the figure is 60, despite increasing use of the morning-after pill, which must be destroying an unknown number of unborn lives. 400,000 prescriptions for this form of emergency contraception were issued last year, women in their late teens or early 20s being the largest group of users.

The 90s have been distinguished by an emphasis on the danger of AIDS, which, though a serious and distressing illness, is in the western world principally connected with homosexual practices and drug addicts sharing needles.

In this book, Valerie Riches' chapter on social engineering describes the changes wrought on family life and British society in recent years. A sea change has occurred in teenagers' attitudes to sexual matters, though not one that has been intended by their parents. Mrs Riches, showing how the sinister side of current policies mainly originated in the eugenic movements of the earlier part of this century, sheds welcome light on what might appear to be an intractable problem.

Professor Melvin Anchell takes a psychoanalytic look at how the development of young children and teenagers is affected by external influences. He shows how sex education threatens normal sexual growth in children and points out that, if left alone, children are normally chaste during puberty. He insists that, while sexual fantasies are a part of growing up, they do not need to be fulfilled, and laments the way in which sex educators encourage their pupils to ignore centuries of wisdom regarding sexual behaviour.

Both Colin Hart's and Paul Atkin's chapters on the laws concerning sex education, and the associated responsibilities of local authorities, will be of great assistance to parents who are concerned about what is being taught at school. There is now a clear role for parents in the running of schools, whether or not they are governors, and they have here an opportunity to learn more about their rights in relation to the sex education of their children. A simple action plan is given in the appendix.

A question was tabled in the House of Lords by Lord Liverpool on 5 March 1992 asking the government whether they considered that 11-year-old children were ready for compulsory and explicit education on HIV and AIDS as required by the *Science in the National Curriculum* document of 1991. The minister replied that because HIV probably constituted the most serious threat to public health this century, children should learn about it once the majority were sufficiently mature to understand its implications. Despite the late Baroness Phillips' intervention that the document included explicit description of oral sex, the minister insisted that factual information could do a good deal to protect young people.

Even if there had been any agreement on the validity of the government's answer, there was no concern expressed for that minority who might not be mature enough to understand the implications. Patricia Morgan's chapter on the subject of AIDS does much to clarify and demystify the excessive attention which has been drawn to this illness, and the way in which it has been used as a pretext for widening the scope of sex education classes to include much more than is needed to give the young a basic understanding of human reproduction.

It is clear from Dr James Le Fanu's chapter on the role of health education that such education can affect the young adversely. As he points out: "The mere knowledge that certain practices might have untoward consequences is not necessarily sufficient incentive to avoid them". Robert Whelan in his penetrating analysis examines the effects of sex education courses on the young and is similarly unable to offer a comforting reply.

The intrinsic value of this publication is that it provides an objective analysis by experts, based on many years of experience and practical considerations in the field of education. Despite the many exhortations for a return to moral values – be they Victorian or those of previous eras – and the noted absence of such values in today's society, the authors' studies are not directed to promoting particular values but to establishing the basic facts which are then scientifically evaluated. The logical analyses in this publication do not seek to support a particular religion or philosophy, but they are deeply concerned with how current educational policies affect the health and behaviour of the young.

Written at a time when truth is too often either stifled or derided, and when only the 'politically correct' tends to be given a hearing, this courageous and valuable work is of great interest and importance.

Editor's note

The chapters of a book with several authors are bound to vary in style, and that is the case with this volume. Indeed, our writers differ in their use of footnotes and other references to sources. We have, however, standardised such references to some extent and placed them after the relevant chapters rather than at the end of the book.

Given the subject of this work, it has been necessary to describe some of the content of sex education materials. We have tried to convey the nature of these publications in a way which, while accurate, is not itself as offensive as the originals. Nevertheless, some readers may find parts of the book unpleasant to read. To them we can only apologise for any distress caused and hope that they understand the need for a work such as this to refer to material which should never have been published, let alone shown to children.

Although this book contains evidence which suggests that sex education can have damaging effects on young people, it is not the intention of the publishers to deprecate the laudable work of those schools where this subject is taught in a sensitive way and in a responsible, family-centred moral context.

Readers are welcome to cite and otherwise reproduce discrete sections of this book, provided that they are quoted in context and fully attributed. Re-publication for sale would, however, require the consent of the copyright owner. Those interested in the work of the Family Education Trust or that of Family & Youth Concern should write to the publisher.

Paul Danon
London, 25 May 1995

1

Sex Education
and Social Engineering

Valerie Riches

Most people would agree that children need to be told properly about human sexuality, rather than being left to find out about it for themselves. Many parents will take comfort from the fact that schools now provide sex education, perhaps believing that they are thus being supported in their parental duty to bring their children to a sensitive understanding of one of the most important aspects of human life.

However, my own family's experience, as well as research that I have done, suggest that sinister motives underlie the sex education movement, and that the content of a lot of sex education is actually hostile to the family values which many parents still support.

First-hand experience

I first became involved in this subject when our son, then aged 14, came home one day from school profoundly shocked, having been subjected to a dose of sex education. At the time, his main interests in life were birds of the feathered variety, not members of the opposite sex. His biology teacher, fresh from a training course run by the Family Planning Association (FPA), had shown a range of contraceptives to an embarrassed class. He told pupils that, since they would probably be going to parties where having sex was *de rigueur*, a means of birth control was indispensable. If, however, a girl nevertheless became pregnant as a result of one of these encounters, an abortion could always be arranged.

15

After my husband and I had complained to the head teacher about this blatant lesson in promiscuity, the biology teacher ostracised our son in front of the rest of the class for having told us. It is hard to imagine anything more likely to silence youngsters than such public intimidation which, we have subsequently learned, is not uncommon. Furthermore, the content of the lesson our son experienced was tame compared with the explicit and amoral sex education now prevalent.

Soon after our son's harrowing experience, our fears were further aroused when a teacher at a sex education symposium in Liverpool boldly proclaimed "we must get into schools, otherwise children will simply follow the *mores* of their parents". What was wrong with our *mores* or those of other average parents, we wondered? We then came across a booklet, *Learning to Live with Sex*, published by the FPA in 1972.[1] Its permissive and amoral text ended with a list of agencies which dealt with birth control, abortion and homosexuality, and the message: "All these places will treat your problems sympathetically and not tell your parents unless you want them to know".

We began to ask questions. Why the profound contempt for parents' *mores*? Why was sex education, unlike other subjects in the curriculum, introduced without the provision of an impartial academic body to assess and evaluate the success or failure of the methodology applied? Why, despite all the sex education and free availability of contraceptives, was the number of teenage pregnancies and abortions rising? How had it all come about? The more we investigated, the more we were astonished by what we discovered and the extent to which we had ourselves been indoctrinated with the prevailing permissive assumptions.

The experience of others

One father wrote to us about a lesson which his 13 year old daughter had attended. "The teacher asked each pupil to write down on paper, without putting their name, as many names – slang or otherwise – for parts of the body, and acts relating to them. As the lists were gone through and discussed, so the depravity of the terms and ideas increased. My wife and I were upset to hear our daughter tell us of the terms that were used, and we felt pain. Some were hideously perverted".

Another parent wrote: "My husband and I are becoming desperately worried about the way our daughter's moral welfare is being taken out of our hands. We feel we are engaged in an unequal struggle with powerful forces that seem intent on indoctrinating her with values that are quite contrary to our own and inappropriate for a child of that age. Before it is too late, and a whole generation of children have been corrupted, some fairly aggressive counter-action needs to be taken".

A school governor has told us about one of three films in the Family Planning Association's *Life Begins* series which was published by the BBC and aimed at 10 and 11 year olds. The film begins with a couple looking at old photographs with their two young children. "Then we go on to a naked family scene where young daughter of approximately three years old runs into her parents' bedroom and tells her mother and father that it is time to get up. The naked mother gets out of bed zombie-like, no smile on her face, and walks down the corridor. The cameras zoom in on the usual areas. She enters the bathroom, washes the child's back in the bath while the cameras continue to home in on the mother's breasts. Back to the bedroom where the zombie father gets out of bed naked; cameras home in again on the usual areas. He goes to the bathroom to shave – no smile – and the cameras continue to home in on him. Then you see a diagram of the male and female reproductive organs.

"The next scene begins with a cartoon of two cats on the roof of a house. The camera takes you inside where there is a 'making love scene' with various things said like: 'it makes the woman feel good all over, ditto the man'. Then we go back to the couple and two small children and there is an array of various contraceptives on the table. The mother says: 'we don't want to have any more children so we use these – some people don't use them for religious reasons'. All dignity is stripped away and I felt tainted and very angry. The headmaster said to us: 'we must flow with the tide'".

The history

For hundreds of years western civilization was basically committed (at least in theory) to an essential link between sex and faithful love in the context of lifelong, monogamous marriage. Children were seen as a blessing – the happy consequence of a fruitful liaison between man and woman. However, these natural assumptions came to be undermined by (among others) the Rev Thomas Malthus in his 1798 *Essay on the Principle of Population*.

Malthus argued that world population would always grow more quickly than the food supply, leading to increased poverty and vice. Charles Darwin came across Malthus' theory and extended the scope of his own work on the animal kingdom to include mankind. Darwin believed that society imperilled itself with misplaced compassion by allowing its weaker members to propagate their kind.

Darwin's cousin, Francis Galton, used Darwin's ideas to formulate the science of eugenics, which is based on the belief that certain human beings are of a superior strain and that the race can be improved by breeding selectively from them. The question the eugenicists asked was "How do you stop those of inferior strains from breeding and damaging the racial stock?" This was the beginning of the birth control movement.

The two most influential campaigners for birth control, Marie Stopes in England and Margaret Sanger in America, were both racists and eugenicists, as well as highly permissive women. Their primary interest consisted of preventing births among groups they considered undesirable. Both women were interested in mass sterilization programmes.

The rise of Nazism in Germany let the eugenicists put their theories into practice, although, after the second world war, they had to abandon their discredited racist claims and instead justify their activities with the new assertion that the world was overpopulated. They also dropped the term birth control, with its fascist connotations, in favour of family planning.

As the birth control movement was modernising itself, the foundations were being laid for the modern sexual revolution.

Kinsey's 1948 *Sexual Behavior in the Human Male* and his 1953 *Sexual Behavior in the Human Female*[2] asserted that there was no such thing as normality or abnormality in sexual relations - no rights or wrongs. Although the validity of Kinsey's sampling techniques was challenged as soon as the first volume had appeared, the media enthusiastically spread the message around the world to the effect that we were entering a period, previously unknown, of undiluted sexual freedom and happiness.

The flaws in Kinsey's method were exposed in *Kinsey, Sex and Fraud, The Indoctrination of a People.*[3] Around one quarter of the male sample had comprised prisoners, including several hundred male prostitutes. Children aged as young as two months had been sexually stimulated to show that sexual activity could be enjoyed from infancy. Data collected from criminal sources was thus presented as serious scientific research and provided the blueprint for sex education policies. It was a breakthrough for the paedophile movement too.

As Kinsey's false conclusions were being increasingly believed, Margaret Sanger founded the Planned Parenthood Federation of America and then, in 1952, started the International Planned Parenthood Federation (IPPF), with headquarters in London. Its eight founder-member associations included the British Family Planning Association. The Population Council in New York was founded by John D. Rockefeller III, who was instrumental in persuading the United Nations to commit itself to population control. Policies devised by these organisations are carried out in each country by IPPF's member bodies around the world.

Typical of the ideology prevailing in the late 1950s were the views propounded in *Can People Learn to Learn?* by Dr Brock Chisholm, first director of the World Health Organisation.[4] Chisholm wanted world government and believed that the most enduring barriers to what he saw as a civilized way of life were the concepts of right and wrong. Codes of belief, fixed rules and dogma were anathema to him. He saw parents as dictators who overruled children's better nature, and believed children should be freed from religious and cultural prejudices that had been forced upon them.

He advocated sex education from an early age and taught that the "ways of elders" should be eliminated, by force if necessary.

Another remarkable book published in 1977, *The SIECUS Circle, A Humanist Revolution*, documented the activities of the Sex Information and Education Council of the United States (SIECUS).[5] This organisation was set up in 1964 and lost no time in engaging in a programme of social engineering by means of sex education in schools. This agency undoubtedly influenced the nature of sex education in schools in the western world. Its first executive director, Mary Calderone, supported the following views expressed in *The Challenge of Marriage* by Rudolph Dreikurs, a humanist:

- that the sexes or sex roles should be merged or reversed;
- that children should be liberated from their families; and,
- that the family should be abolished as we have known it.

These radical ideas were embedded in policies, programmes and publications, and have been spread throughout the world to unsuspecting populations and governments by means of sex education programmes and publications promoted by the IPPF through its world-wide member-bodies.

In 1976, the IPPF set out its 'Strategy of Legal Reform' which urged its member-organisations to identify areas of law which could be reformed and to find arguments for such reforms.[6] Reforms under the heading of the "status of women" included the promotion of family planning, abortion and sterilization. There were also to be tax reforms, relaxed divorce and family laws, a lower age of consent for birth control services "to meet the needs of young people", and, inevitably, compulsory sex education.

An IPPF report, *The Human Right to Family Planning*, published in 1984, stated that children from the age of 10 should have full access to fertility regulation, and to information and services, with guaranteed privacy and confidentiality - that is, without the consent of parents.[7] With a total lack of self-doubt and apparently confident that the IPPF was above the law, the report states: "Family planning associations and other non-governmental organisations should not use the absence of law or the existence of an unfavourable law as an excuse for inaction; action outside the law and even in violation of it is part of the process of stimulating change". Another IPPF report, *A Strategy for Legal Change*, showed how, in Togo, the FPA had achieved sex education in schools in contravention of existing laws.[8]

The effects

In the 1950s, before sex education became widespread, there were just a few hundred pregnancies among the under-16s in Britain each year. By the 1990s, the number of such pregnancies had risen to nearly 9,000 – the highest in Europe – even though sex education and contraception had become widely available. The Brook Advisory Centres' researcher concedes: "There is overwhelming evidence that, contrary to what you might expect, the availability of contraception leads to an increase in the abortion rate".[9]

Population control groups openly admit that the main influence on couples' attitudes to fertility is not the availability of contraception or abortion but the culture in which they live. Since most cultures are centred on the family, the birth control movement must make family life in developing countries conform to the assumptions and values of modern western consumer societies. For example, people must be persuaded that sex and marriage, and sex and childbearing, do not necessarily go together; that extra-marital cohabitation is a viable, even desirable, option; and that children have a right to their own sex lives without interference from their parents.

When such attitudes are adopted, birth rates fall, hence the attack on the family which always forms part of population control programmes and hence IPPF's interest in apparently peripheral issues such as taxation, women's liberation, marriage and divorce and, crucially, the sex education of children.

Agents of change in the UK

Because public education is an affair of the state, the advocates of sex education support, above all else, an expansion of the scope of state intervention in the sex education of children. This view was put succinctly in 1980 by Lady Helen Brook, the president and founder of the Brook Advisory Centres, in a letter responding to critics of explicit sex education: "From birth till death it is now the privilege of the parental state to take major decisions - objective, unemotional, the state weighs up what is best for the child".[10]

A policy statement issued by the Family Planning Association (FPA) in 1978 stated that sex education should " . . . provide an incentive to work towards a society in which archaic sex laws, irrational fears of sex and sexual exploitation are non-existent".[11] This is confirmed in much of the FPA's resource material for schools.

A popular book among sex educators is *Make it Happy*, first published by Virago in 1978.[12] It is a battering-ram for breaking down social constraints and taboos. Adolescent children are given information on how to have sex in every possible way, including activity which cannot by its nature result in pregnancy such as anal and oral sex, and bestiality short of penetration.

The book, and others like it, asserts that feelings of revulsion against perversions, and any sense of guilt, must be overcome. There is only one moral absolute: a method of birth control must be used every time sexual intercourse takes place, safe in the knowledge that parents will not be told.

Sex educators want to start with children while they are young. In 1970 a spokesman for the FPA's education department said to a government committee: "Contraceptive education has to be given very young. It is almost too late when the children get to puberty . . . children in schools are a captive audience".[13]

The FPA's *Primary School Work Book*, published in 1993, has the subtitle *Teaching sex education within the National Curriculum* and is aimed at four to 11 year olds.[14] It includes a "sexual activity word puzzle" in which children must look at a jumble of letters and find, in this order: massage, cuddle, sexual intercourse, gay, hug, sex, kiss, lick, laugh, touch and lesbian. The clear message of the book is that heterosexuality is just one option and it encourages children to masturbate alone and with others. "Sole and mutual masturbation", they are told, "is now encouraged as part of safer sex".

In 1994 the FPA organised a highly-publicised visit to Britain by a SIECUS team which aimed to counter attempts to promote chastity by such groups as CARE and Family & Youth Concern. The team warned that the promotion of chastity would lead to fear and guilt. The FPA also ran a 1994 conference at the Royal Society of Arts, London, funded by Organon, the contraceptive pill manufacturer. Speakers included the BBC's Ms Jenni Murray, who has denounced marriage, and Ms Suzie Hayman, author of *Say Yes? Say No? Say Maybe?* which includes a 'Good Grope Guide'.[15] Other participants were Mr Nick Fisher, agony uncle of *Just 17* magazine and author of *Your Pocket Guide to Sex*, copies of which were ordered by a health minister to be shredded; Ms Helen Christopher of the HEA, which published Mr Fisher's book; as well as a lesbian who spoke on the politics of parenting.

The FPA has an annual budget of more than £2.5 million, of which more than one third comes from government grants. As well as having a fund-raising arm, Population Concern, it also receives the profits from FP Sales Ltd, "an independently operated company" established in 1972 which sells contraceptives. The FPA's activities boost not only the profits of FP Sales but also those of other companies. The 1975 Monopolies & Mergers Commission report on contraceptive sheaths quotes a representative of London Rubber Industries as saying that the FPA's educational activities "widen the market for contraceptives".[16] It would be interesting to know what the commission would say now that AIDS has further enlarged the condom market.

It is interesting to note that the Health Education Authority, a government quango, declined to include in its resource list a video aimed at teenagers entitled *The Truth About AIDS* published by the Family Education Trust. The reason given for this was that it did not comply with the Chief Medical Officer's policy on AIDS prevention, that is, the promotion of the condom. The message in the video is that to prevent the spread of the disease the only safe sex is chaste sex. Yet the HEA included in its resource list an amoral and obscene video *The Gay Man's Guide to Safer Sex*, produced by Pride Video Productions and the Terrence Higgins

Trust. This video shows the practicalities of safer sex and contains explicit demonstrations of male sexual activity.[17]

The Brook Advisory Centres, which receive government grants, are very active in providing teenage contraceptive clinics around the country, as well as grossly permissive sex education. The following advice is typical of its approach: "Get over your giggles by using condoms . . . and getting used to them. Blow them up at parties - see who can burst theirs first or who gets them biggest . . . Girls can practise opening a packet and putting them on their partners (use a banana as a model) and boys can practise putting them on and wanking . . . try it on your own and you'll soon become an expert".[18]

These organisations and other connected interests bitterly oppose any attempts to restore parental responsibility for the sex lives of their children. At the time of writing outrage is being expressed that parents now have the right in law to withdraw their children from sex education which may offend their religious and philosophical beliefs.

The future

Family breakdown in the UK is a matter of grave social concern. We have the highest divorce and illegitimacy rate in Europe. Cohabitation is increasing and marriage rates are falling.[19] There is a corresponding rise in crime and in the sexual and physical abuse of children: more broken homes mean more battered children.

In *The Health of the Nation* the British government committed itself to halving the number of teenage pregnancies by the year 2000, not by promoting chastity but by giving more explicit sex education to younger and younger children, and by promoting post-coital contraception.[20] The government has been persuaded by the sex education lobby's claim that widespread promotion of contraception through explicit sex education in the Netherlands has led to that country's having the lowest teenage pregnancy rate in Europe. However, in a 1990 letter which was accompanied by an enclosure concerning the Dutch Abortion Act, the Secretary of State for Welfare, Public Health and Culture described a type of abortion known as menstrual extraction (ME).[21] This process of instrumental abortion can be carried out up to 16 days after a woman's (or a girl's) period has become overdue, and as long as 44 days after the previous menstruation.

The Secretary of State's letter pointed out that: "ME – not coming under the law – does not take place in licensed clinics. This way ME is taken out of control and moreover, in unlicensed clinics, under the flag of ME, older foetuses will easily be aborted without the inspectorate . . . having a hold on it". Since terminations of teenage pregnancies in cases of ME are not registered as abortions, the actual number of teenage pregnancies in the Netherlands must greatly exceed official figures.

Summary

Sex education in schools was not introduced in response to public demand. There was no parental lobby clamouring for it. The demand came, rather, from a lobby of sexual revolutionaries – enterprising businessmen and researchers who convinced policy-makers and the media that sex education in schools would help children avoid the pitfalls of adolescence.

The principal responsibility of parents is to ensure that children learn the truth and that means more than giving physical facts. It means helping children to understand that there are rights and wrongs. It involves deeper questions about the true significance of human sexuality: what giving oneself in sexual intercourse means; and the effect that such giving can have on one's inner being and that of one's partner. Sex education ought to help buttress children against the sexual excesses of modern society. It should teach children that each individual has an intellect, a will and intrinsic value. It should help children understand that each person is engaged in a life-long struggle for self-mastery, in which the will and intellect wisely control the sensual appetites.

However, sex education of the kind described in this chapter undermines the consciences of children by encouraging the indiscriminate pursuit of personal pleasure, and therefore militates against the family. Parents, school governors and pupils themselves should not be afraid to challenge the authority of individuals or prestigious bodies who offer publications, visual aids, training courses, and school programmes. It is worth asking questions about such material. Is it commercially orientated? What are the aims and motives of those producing it? Is the content compliant with policy guidelines issued by the Department for Education and the various Education Acts?

The reality of the history, aims and practices of the sex education lobby will come as a shock to many parents and policy makers. Some may indeed find it difficult to credit. Yet the truth must be told: apparently worthy national and international organisations funded by governments have interests in the sex education of our children as the means by which to spread an amoralism that is hostile to the family and the sanctity of human life. The sex education movement has been described as "one of the most savagely damaging lobbies a society has ever had to confront".[22] The welfare of children of this and future generations is at stake. The stability of the family and the very future of the human race is under grave threat. It is therefore imperative that people of goodwill face up to this threat with energy and vigour.

Notes

1   *Learning to Live with Sex*, FPA, 1972 (first edition).

2   A.C.Kinsey, *Sexual Behavior in the Human Male*, Saunders, Pa., 1948; *Sexual Behavior in the Human Female*, Saunders, Pa., 1953.

3   Judith A.Reisman and E.W.Eichel, *Kinsey, Sex and Fraud, The Indoctrination of a People*, edited by John H. Court and J. Gordon Muir, Huntingdon House, 1990.

4   Brock Chisholm, *Can People Learn to Learn?* George Allen and Unwin, London, 1958.

5 Claire Chambers, *The SIECUS Circle, A Humanist Revolution*, Western Islands, 1977.

6 'Strategy for Legal Reform and How FPAs are Interpreting It', *IPPF News*, July/August 1976.

7 The Human Right to Family Planning, IPPF, London, 1984.

8 *A Strategy for Legal Change*, IPPF, London, 1981.

9 'Sex Education for Bureaucrats', Judith Bury, *The Scotsman*, 29 June 1981.

10 Helen Brook, letter to *The Times*, 16 February 1980.

11 'Sex Education, an FPA Statement', August 1974.

12 Jane Cousins, *Make It Happy*, Virago, 1978 (first edition).

13 Minutes of Evidence on Population, Select Committee on Science and Technology, HMSO, 1970.

14 Gill Lenderyou, *Primary School Work Book*, FPA, London, 1993.

15 *Say Yes? Say No? Say Maybe?* Brook Advisory Centres, 1991.

16 *Contraceptive Sheaths: A Report on the Supply of Contraceptive Sheaths in the United Kingdom*, The Monopolies and Mergers Commission, HMSO, 1975.

17 *HIV and AIDS, Supplementary Resource List*, Health Education Authority, Autumn 1992.

18 *Say Yes? Say No? Say Maybe?* Brook Advisory Centres, 1991.

19 George Brown, *The Decay of Marriage*, Family Education Trust, 1991.

20 *Health of the Nation: A Strategy of Health for England.* Cm Paper 1986. H.M.S.O., London, 1992.

21 Letter and enclosures, Hans J Simons, Secretary of State for Welfare, Public Health and Culture, The Hague, Holland, May 1990.

22 Patrick Cosgrave, 'The Politics of Sex Education', *The Spectator*, August 1974.

2

Pre-Teen and Teenage Sex and Environmental Influences

Melvin Anchell

This chapter is based on a paper presented in Brighton at the XVIth International Congress for the Family, 1990

The topic of my paper is a psychoanalytic look at some environmental influences - especially school sex education - that affect pre-teen and teenage sexual behaviour.

The facts to be presented are based on established psychoanalytic principles, my personal observations of young patients whom I have treated psychoanalytically, the case histories of other clinical investigators, and any source of data that can be clinically substantiated with everyday patients.

My discussion will first consider some environmental influences affecting 10-12 year old sexual behaviour and will follow with the effect of these influences on the sexual behaviour of pubertal and adolescent youth.

A distinctive characteristic seen in 10-12 year old children is an increase in activity to adjust to the realities of the adult world. This increase in activity in 10-12 year olds to adapt to grown-up realities differs markedly in boys and girls. In the boy, his adaptations to adult realities are directed outward, towards his environs, giving him an objective aggressiveness which the male uses throughout life to master the environment and to achieve utilitarian goals. In girls, their increased activity to become grown-up is directed inward, towards the psyche, that is, their minds.

Pre-pubertal boys' and girls' activities directed to becoming independent and grown-up are greatly influenced by identification with parents, family values and standards, and consciences instilled in the minds of young people by parents.

However, when the 10-12 year old reaches the age of 13, that is puberty, psychological changes occur which push parental influences into the background, and identifications with individuals outside the home begin to play major roles in influencing the behaviour of teenagers.

If environmental influences are in accord with the previous parental teachings, new adaptations to life are made harmoniously, and pubertal-adolescent maturation progresses smoothly into early adulthood. When, however, the environment is 'out of sync' with parental teachings, parents and the child's conscience are rapidly deprecated in the minds of most youths. Under such circumstances, leaders in the contravening environment replace the authority of parents, and the consciences of young people are decimated by the beliefs and teachings of new leaders.

In the sexual development of 10-12 year old children, secrecy and curiosity, which are loosely attached filaments of the human sexual instinct, provide the sensual pleasures normal for this age group. In girls, sensual gratification derived from secrecy and curiosity is shared with other girls of the same age. The clandestine secrets of pre-pubertal girls are always investigated privately before sharing the findings with a girlfriend. The privacy used in acquiring sexual information is a first step in life leading to individuality and independence.

Pleasures derived from sharing secrets with other girls are the only pre-pubertal sensual activity. In all other respects, the 10-12 year old girl friendships are normally non-sexual. The privately investigated secrets concern psychological sexual matters and are not related to sex with boys. Sex between girls and boys normally plays no part in the lives of 10-12 year old children. Pre-pubertal boys regard close friendships with girls as unmanly; and girls adopt an 'I don't care' attitude.

Today's school sex education given to pre-pubertal children completely shatters the normal sexual secrecy pleasures and compassionate girl friendships by catapulting 10-12 year olds into a world of ready-made, instant sexual information. Such school interferences usurp girl-to-girl friendships with their harmless sensual secrets, and at the same time disrupt the beginning development of individualism and independence.

Many acts of gangsterism, prostitution and criminality in 10-12 year old children result from the violent interruption of normal pre-teen sexual growth with premature sex acts foisted by school sex teachings. Since the advent of school sex education, promiscuity, pregnancies and venereal diseases are no longer uncommon in 10-12 year old children.

Almost invariably pubertal and teen youths separated into two parts by family and environmental differences will develop, in some degree, attitudes offensive to the family. For example, youths brought up in sexually moral homes become critical of the family when taking school sex courses that glorify all types of physical sex while at the same time 'damning by faint praise' the affectionate nature of human sexuality stressed by parents.

School sex courses at all grade levels can teach one thing only, and that is physical sex. The vitally important, life-sustaining affectionate component of human sexuality cannot be learned from a school textbook. Unfortunately, notwithstanding family allegiances, teenagers all too often favour the school sex teachings, making it almost impossible for them to make sexually mature adjustments in later life.

By the age of 13, prepubertal girl-to-girl friendships gradually lessen as the girls grow older and go their separate ways. Puberty is also a time when sexual energies that have remained dormant during the latency years of 6-12 are once again reawakened. The reawakened sexual energies of pubertal boys are direct and are centered on the male genitalia. The reawakened eroticism of 13 year old girls follow a much different course.

Because teenage female biological and psychological maturations are not completed until late adolescence, and because female genitalia remains anaesthetic to anatomical sex until at least late

31

adolescence, nature has provided the young girl with a natural aversion to the sex act. Contrary to the teachings of sex educators, both sexes - if left undisturbed by school sex teachings and the pornographically orientated entertainment media - are normally chaste during puberty and adolescence.

Although the teenage girl has a natural aversion to engaging in the sex act, her sexual desires may nevertheless be as intense as the boy's. Teenage female eroticisms involve the desire to love and be loved, kisses and caresses, tender words of love, sexual fantasies, and sometimes thoughts of pregnancy and motherhood. But unlike the male, the girl's sexual eroticisms are not inseparably entwined with the sex act.

The dichotomy between the adolescent boy's capability for the sex act and the girl's natural reluctance to sexual intercourse may seem strange, but nature always has a reason for what it does. The teenage girl's reluctance to the sex act serves to strengthen the affectionate and spiritual nature of sex. Through affection and sexual spiritualisation, both sexes learn to regard sex and the sex partner with the utmost importance.

Spiritualisation of sex leads to the idealisation of members of the opposite sex. Idealisation of a special someone makes life complete. The answer is not that 1 plus 1 equals 2, but that ½ plus ½ make one whole person. This is the basis for monogamous love which forms the foundation for western civilization.

It should be noted that sexual fantasies are important for adolescent sexual development. The fantasies primarily consist of an ardent desire for love with someone of the opposite sex. Such fantasies are natural, beneficial, and gratifying, but they are not meant to be carried out in real life.

To paraphrase the impression of many sexually-educated youths: 'if they are teaching it to us in school, then they are telling us to go ahead and have sex - for what other reason are they giving out free condoms?'

It should be clearly understood that under usual environmental circumstances, teenagers are normally chaste, preferring to engage in platonic relationships. Some reasons given by youths for becoming sexually active in today's world are to prove that they are grown-ups, to surpass older siblings and friends, to gain prestige from classmates by engaging in school-condoned sex, to take revenge on parents who are accused of thwarting independence, and to take advantage of the sexual permissiveness overlooked by schools.

Another school sex education related catastrophe is the ever-increasing numbers of adolescent lesbians in the United States. Students in sex classes are taught that all perversions are normal.

Given this assurance, some disappointed girls, who find no gratification in genital intercourse, and feel they have been used and abused by providing indifferent males with sexual satisfaction, turn once again to the more earnest girl-to-girl friendships they recall from prepubertal years. However, exclusive relationships between adolescent girls - devoid of boys - differ from the 10-12 year old girl friendships. Erotic feelings are more intense during adolescence, and may push girls into homosexual activities which arrest further heterosexual development.

The greatest harm done by today's school sex education is that all sex courses, from kindergarten through high school, destroy natural sexual growth. In human beings, unlike any other creatures, three phases of sexual development occur before adult sexual maturity is reached. The first phase of human sexual development occurs at birth and lasts through the fifth year of life; the second phase begins at six and continues through the age of twelve; and the third phase of human sexual development starts at puberty around the age of thirteen and is not completed until late adolescence.

Sex education proponents are resolute in their resolve to involve themselves in the sexual development of children and young people, and to inculcate physical sexual matters into youths' minds. The illiterate sexual intermeddlings of sex teachers in the developing sexuality of children and youths could actually be considered comical if it weren't for the egregious harm that is done to students and society.

The sex 'educators' have no compunction in overriding any data that is not supportive of their sex education theories. For example, a recent international survey on approximately 30,000 thirteen year old students from a number of nations clearly showed 'American students come out at the bottom of the heap scholastically . . . and revealed a marked weakness in higher-order thinking skills . . .'

Such research is disregarded by sex educators who insist that "immature juvenile students" formulate new sexual standards and values and use their own judgement in determining whether or not to engage in sex - and if so, what sex acts to commit.

In developing new standards and values, the students are implicitly or openly cautioned not to heed thousands of years of tried and tested life sustaining findings, nor pay attention to teachings of parents, because these sources - students are made to believe - are prejudiced, puritanical, outdated, and erroneous. Instead, students are taught to rely on the "sex is for fun" transgressions of Planned Parenthood, and on the sexual propaganda of homosexual activists.

Sexually educated young people are not a new breed of youths who, under the guiding patronage of a progressive educational system, have managed in one generation to change five thousand years of human sexuality.

The new breed simply represents misled children who have been rushed into 'sham sex' by benighted sex educators. Parents and the public may listen and even see, but rarely can anyone who attended school prior to today's sex education possibly fathom how deeply sex-educated young people have been led into wanton sex. For example, recently a major Chicago newspaper casually reported that 80% of freshmen to senior female students in a Chicago high school are pregnant. Can any parent over thirty truly imagine what is happening in education to create such disasters?

By some means or other, sex teachers in the United States, under the auspices of SIECUS and Planned Parenthood, have summarily seized the right to teach children and youths how to mate in every way, how to override inborn mental barriers against perversions, how to rely on contraceptives and abortions, and how to engage in all sex acts without guilt. These are the characteristics of pimps and prostitutes.

To justify their coup, educators frequently use the argument that parents don't feel comfortable teaching sex to children and prefer to leave such matters to school teachers. At the same time, some teachers complain that they are being imposed upon by parents - especially those parents who expect schools to uphold Judaeo-Christian sexual morality - a morality, incidentally, that supports the struggle for existence, sustains civilized lives, is in line with all enduring religions, and is a morality whose life-sustaining nature is substantiated by psychoanalytic observations.

At no time do educators remotely explain who decided, and for what reason, it became suddenly fashionable to teach physical sex and perversions to school children living in the late 20th century!

Aside from evading these questions, sex educators shun the fundamental psychoanalytical facts that unequivocally show school sex education from kindergarten to 12 causes irreparable harm to students throughout life. For example, when the psychoanalytic fact became widely known that sex education destroys sexual growth and personal development during the latency years of six to 12, Mary Calderone, the leader of SIECUS, simply decreed that the latency period did not exist. Subsequently, followers of SIECUS and Planned Parenthood dismissed from further consideration the pernicious harm done to six to 12 year old children by school sex teachings.

Not only do sex educators disregard scientific psychoanalytic knowledge, but when it suits their purpose, they likewise turn their backs to the findings of their very own principal sex investigators. For example, Alfred Kinsey is one of the sex educators' 'leading lights'. In his sex questionnaire studies, Kinsey found and reported that the average female had an intense aversion for engaging in the sex act. Nevertheless, his finding is rejected by sex educators, and students in sex classes are taught that it is usual and gratifying for young girls to engage in sexual intercourse. To avoid appearing abnormal and rebuffed by their classmates, many female students arrange to lose their virginity to someone when they become fourteen.

Another 'guiding light' sexologist highly used by Planned Parenthood sex educators is Dr William Masters. SIECUS's Mary Calderone virtually deified Masters for his sexual experiments in which he used prostitutes, as well as paid and unpaid volunteers. Recently however, Dr Masters must have had a change of heart for he denounced homosexuality and homosexual acts in a magazine article.

An ostentatious cliché used by proponents of school sex education is: 'If they don't learn it at school, they'll learn it on the street anyway'. Such justification for teaching children carnality is as logical as trying to control a fire by dumping more fuel on the flames.

It is true that there are 'street smart' pubertal girls who not infrequently become trapped into sex acts by identifying with sexually loose older females and by emulating sexually uninhibited heroines seen in many of today's movies and television shows. But sex education is not the solution for these young girls who play out their provocative coquetry on the street and who feel secure because they realise that they have no real desire for sexual intercourse. However, when their seductive coquetishness becomes too intense, it may free some men from any scruples they have concerning a juvenile.

In this way, all too often, 12, 13 and 14 year old girls, who frequently make themselves look older, encounter their first sex experience. The first experience is, not infrequently, followed by others on the basis of the girl's feeling: 'Well, now everything has been lost anyhow - what is there to lose?'

Some sexually active girls regret their sexual involvements, but nevertheless continue sexual offences against themselves as a form of self-punishment. Prostitution, venereal diseases, or illegitimate children are frequent consequences of their remorse.

A generally known psychoanalytic fact concerning human sexuality is that the female is prone to follow the conventions of her culture. If her social order regards chastity as a virtue, she becomes chaste. If her society espouses free love, she may readily assume the characteristics of a promiscuous woman.

The brusque truth is that today's sexually emancipated female is not an example of 'new progressive social changes which have made her a free individual'. She simply represents a woman - or girl - who has become a slave to the demands of her society.

Some girls resist this sexual enslavement by returning to their families. School teachers frequently label such girls as 'immature and family dependent', but in reality these chaste young females develop into fully mature women who become ideal spouses, mothers and home makers.

Conversely, some other girls accept the sexual expectations society makes upon them, and take on the characteristics of the male's sexual aggressiveness. Many rush hungrily from one man to another and learn to equate love with fornication. Such females keep searching for the 'Grand Passion' all their lives - even when they are happily married.

A variety of subconscious defence mechanisms are used by many modern females to fend off the sexual flummery imposed upon them. For example, some girls turn to intellectualism as a means of defence. This particular defence reaction against sexual impositions may seem sound, but unfortunately, intellectualism - unless the girl is born with a surfeit of intellectuality - feeds upon the affective life of feminacy. That is, a girl's intellectualism or objectivism gets much of its energy from female emotions, leaving her largely depleted of rich, warm feminine feelings.

Other defence reactions against unwanted anatomical sex can be seen in girls who excel in sports, take up professions and business careers, become activists in various ideological or political groups, or join communes or cults as a means of escape. However, sports, play, work and intellectual pursuits are not adequate substitutes for a close, emotional relationship with a person of the opposite sex.

The goal of a boy should be to become a man and that of a girl to become a woman. The development of the feminine woman involves female maturation processes that are not completed until late adolescence.

Premature sex during adolescence disrupts natural feminine maturation, as does too early a motherhood. The demands made upon a young teenage girl by pregnancy require that she use all her energies for the pregnancy and for the caring of a newborn child. Infantile mothers fail to develop real motherliness, even under the most favourable conditions, and a too early motherhood leaves little physical energy for developing the girl's personality which remains incomplete.

In humans, unlike animals, when affectionate needs are not met and physical sex is all that remains, sex becomes meaningless and life becomes empty. This psychoanalytic maxim is readily apparent in the suicides of 'sexually educated, sexually active' youths. Suicide now ranks as the leading cause of death in young people under the age of 21 in the United States.

Over the past 25 years or so, a sexual revolution has been destroying western civilization by vilifying human sexuality. The effects have been truly devastating. Assuming this scourge has not, as yet, brought us to the point of no return, what can be done?

First, I believe, society must re-establish its social conscience, a conscience that – as just a generation ago – will not sanction free love and perversions, will not permit gutter sex to be spread publicly by pornographically orientated media, and will not tolerate schools acting as sex abusers.

Sexual revolutionists, by corrupting the meaning of 'free speech' and by stretching the boundaries of sexual indecency, are persuading much of the public into accepting social degeneracy. Fortunately, however, civilization is not a one way street. Restoration of a social conscience can not only stop the decline of our civilization, but also help it climb back out of the abyss into which it has been flung by those determined to make western society a bastion for pagan sexual hedonism.

In conclusion, two matters stand out. Firstly, life-sustaining sex completely depends on an affectionate, monogamous, long lasting, love relationship between a man and a woman. Such relationships are essential for the survival of civilizations based on families composed of individuals living by conscience, instead of barbarians living by instincts only. Secondly, for the benefit of all mankind, it is just as important to eradicate the psychological venereal diseases that are rife today as it is to eradicate physical venereal diseases, such as AIDS. Both arise from the malignant abuse of human sexuality.

3

The Law on Sex Education

Colin Hart

Geographical note: this chapter deals chiefly with the law on sex education in state-supported schools in England and Wales. Such law applies to sixth formers in schools but not to students at institutions such as sixth-form colleges. There is no legislation on sex education which applies to state schools in Scotland (although the 1986 Local Government Act deals in part with sex education and this Act applies in Scotland) nor any which applies to British independent schools.

Parliament first intervenes

During the 1980s the practice of offering sex education in secondary schools became almost universal. In some schools it was taught in science lessons and in others it was part of personal and social education. However, the legal framework governing such lessons took some time to be established.

The 1980 Education Act began by requiring local education authorities (LEAs) to tell parents of the manner and context in which any sex education was given, though it gave no guidelines on content.[1] Next, the 1986 Education (No.2) Act made governing bodies draw up a sex education policy (which could consist of offering no sex education) and to consider representations from the community and senior police officers. Parents could ask to have their children excused from sex education, but governors could decline such requests.[2]

The 1986 Act required that sex education was given in such a way "as to encourage those pupils to have due regard to moral considerations and the value of family life" (section 46) and this requirement remains in force.

Guidance on content

The following year the Department for Education and Science (DES) issued further guidance in circular 11/87, whose measured tone is reflected in the following quotations:

> The aim of a programme of sex education should be . . . to enable pupils . . . to know what is and is not legal.[3]

> Pupils should be encouraged to consider the importance of self-restraint, dignity and respect for themselves and others, and helped to recognise the physical, emotional and moral risks of casual and promiscuous sexual behaviour. Pupils should be helped to appreciate the benefits of stable married and family life and the responsibilities of parenthood.[4]

> There is no place in any school in any circumstances for teaching which advocates homosexual behaviour, which presents it as the norm . . .'[5]

The DES also expected schools to stress to their pupils the requirements of the law on the age of consent, homosexuality and indecent assault.[6] The government thus laid the foundations for a fairly responsible approach to sex education.

Gay Lessons: the promotion of homosexuality

Shortly after the 1986 Act had gained royal assent Miss Rachel Tingle, the journalist, published a study entitled *Gay Lessons* which showed how public funds were being used to promote homosexuality amongst young people.[7]

The Greater London Council (GLC, since abolished) had given more than £1 million to gay groups and promoted the use of very explicit material which encouraged homosexual experimentation. The GLC made grants to such organisations as Gayman's Press which published *Jenny lives with Eric and Martin*, a lavishly illustrated book for five to seven year olds portraying a homosexual family where a five year old lives with two homosexual lovers.

Although an official of the Inner London Education Authority (ILEA) defended the publication as "an aid for teachers working in personal and social development with children", controversy in the national press led to the ILEA withdrawing the booklet.[8] Miss Tingle's research showed, however, that many pro-gay resources were nevertheless being used by LEAs and youth services. Homosexual families were portrayed as normal and homosexual experimentation was being encouraged by videos and textbooks.

Although the Earl of Halsbury and Dame Jill Knight MP failed in the spring of 1987 with their private bill to stop such homosexual proselytism, the following year the earl successfully amended the Local Government Bill to prevent councils from promoting homosexual activities. His Clause 28 inserted section 2A in the 1986 Local Government Act, which remains in force and also applies to Scotland. Section 2A reads:

1. A local authority shall not

    (a) intentionally promote homosexuality or publish material with the intention of promoting homosexuality;
    (b) promote the teaching in any maintained school of the acceptability of homosexuality as a pretended family relationship

2. Nothing in subsection (1) above shall be taken to prohibit the doing of anything for the purpose of treating or preventing the spread of disease . . .

The Act thus allowed local authorities to promote homosexuality under the pretence of preventing the spread of HIV.

Sex education as part of the national curriculum

In 1991 the Government added teaching on HIV and other sexual diseases to the science national curriculum for 11 to 14 year olds, which already included teaching on puberty, sexual reproduction and the need for a responsible attitude to sexual behaviour.[9] This gave further encouragement to the sex education industry and led to the production of some of the most explicit and unhelpful materials, including resources from the DES.[10]

The change to the science national curriculum also went against the 1986 Act by removing governors' powers to let parents have their children excused. A value-free approach to sex education was encouraged and behaviour associated with a high HIV risk was presented in a neutral fashion. The science national curriculum did not acknowledge the 1986 Act's requirements for a moral and family context for sex, which applied only to sex education taught according to governors' policies.

Gathering parental concern

In the early 1990s some LEAs' policies became yet more extreme. The danger of AIDS was used to justify very explicit sex education, such as getting children to put condoms on carrots. Obscene language was considered a good way of putting pupils at their ease when discussing sexual behaviour, and parents with objections to such a value-free approach could not withdraw their children.

Groups of parents lobbied Parliament and, in June 1993, after two full-scale debates[11] in the House of Lords, Lord Stallard moved an amendment to the Education Bill. The amendment looked like succeeding and was only withdrawn when Baroness Blatch, an education minister, promised a Government amendment during the Bill's third reading.

The 1993 Education Act

The 1993 Education Act made the distinction between science lessons dealing with human reproduction and other sex education. It required the Secretary of State to issue an order prohibiting, within the science national curriculum, teaching on:

(a) AIDS, and HIV;

(b) any other sexually transmitted disease; or,

(c) aspects of human sexual behaviour other than biological aspects.[12]

Parents may not withdraw their children from science lessons dealing with human sexuality.

The Act also gave responsibility for other types of sex education back to governing bodies and, for the first time, required secondary schools to provide sex education (in addition to that given in science lessons). Such lessons must:

include education about

(a) AIDS, HIV and

(b) any other sexually transmitted diseases.[13]

Before the Act, HIV had to be studied by the age of 14, but the Act allows the postponement of the subject until after 14. Parents can withdraw their children from the sex education provided as part of governors' responsibilities and all such teaching must be presented in the moral and family-centred context described in section 46 of the 1986 Education Act, which still applies. Primary school governors are free to decide to have no sex education taught at all (except that taught in science).

At the time of writing, it appears that Sir Ron Dearing's slimming down of the national curriculum will not stop children from having to cover human development and reproduction at primary school, and that 11 to 14 year olds will continue to study puberty and human reproduction.[14]

Government guidance after the 1993 Act

In May 1994 Mr John Patten, the Secretary of State for Education, hailed the guidance on sex education in Circular 5/94 as a return to traditional values, but the reality was quite different. During the drafting of the circular, pro-family statements were reduced to a politically correct fudge and last-minute attempts by MPs to strengthen the circular were only partially successful.

The guidance is vague on important issues. At draft stage a sentence about helping pupils "to appreciate the benefits of stable married and family life and the responsibilities of parenthood"[15] was changed to describe helping them "appreciate the value of stable family life, marriage and the responsibilities of parenthood".[16] The final wording implies that stable family life is possible without marriage. Since the science national curriculum is exempt from this requirement, parents who see marriage as the only proper context for sex could well be concerned at an amoral presentation of the subject.

A letter-writing campaign by Stonewall, the gay lobby group, led to the removal from the circular of statements forbidding the promotion of homosexuality.[17] Mr Peter Tatchell, the gay-rights campaigner, was quoted as saying that schools would be able to take a tougher line against anti-gay prejudice.[18] Circular 5/94 also pointed out that Clause 28 applied to LEAs and not to schools themselves,[19] the implication being that, as long as the LEA was not involved, schools could promote homosexuality.

Parental rights

Parents have considerably more legal rights than they did before the 1988 and 1993 Education Acts. A judicious exercise of those rights could have a considerable influence on governors as they draw up plans for sex education. Circular 5/94 can be cited to raise important points with schools about sensitivity to parents' wishes. Parental rights fall into four areas:

1. The right to know

Parents have a legal right to a free copy of the school's sex education policy,[20] a summary of which must be included in the free school prospectus.[21] Parents can also have a copy of any syllabus used by teachers ("a work scheme"),[22] but schools may charge for photocopying. Parents can see copies of textbooks and other resources for sex education.

2. The right to complain

Informal. If parents are concerned, or just wish to enquire, about the content of sex education, they should initially see the headteacher. Although most complaints can be resolved with politeness, firmness and persistence, a parent may subsequently choose to contact the elected parent governor(s) and/or the chairman of governors. Local councillors can also be lobbied. It is more effective for a number of parents to join together in making a complaint.

Formal. Section 23 of the 1988 Education Reform Act allows parents of pupils in local authority schools to complain about any aspect of the school curriculum, though not about individual teachers. A copy of the procedure can be obtained from schools. A parent who complains is given the right to present their case in person. The complaint is first dealt with by the governing body and, if the complainant is not satisfied, by the LEA. If, after the LEA has given its ruling, the matter has still not been resolved, there is the right to appeal to the Secretary of State on one of two grounds:

- that, under section 68 of the 1944 Education Act, the governing body has acted unreasonably;
- that, under section 99 of the 1944 Act, a governing body or LEA has failed to fulfil its statutory duties.

The Secretary of State will only consider complaints once the local procedure has been completed.

In the academic year 1990-91, only four out of a total of 75 complaints under the procedure were about sex education. There is evidence of widespread ignorance amongst parents of the procedures.[23] The grant-maintained schools also have complaints procedures which resemble those for LEA schools.[24]

3. The right of withdrawal

The parental right of withdrawal now applies regardless of whether the school agrees with parents' exercising this right. Parents do not have to give any reason for wishing their child to be withdrawn, neither do they have any obligation to give their children sex education at home.[25] It is sensible for parents to make the request in writing.

The withdrawal can be total or partial; parents may list the topics from which their children are to be excused. The right of withdrawal does not extend to biological aspects of human sexual behaviour and reproduction which remain part of the compulsory science national curriculum.

Sex education taught in science lessons could lead to confusion since a parental right of withdrawal exists for sex education, but not for the biological aspects within science. The right of withdrawal from sex education remains, irrespective of how it is taught.

4. The right to be consulted

Schools' governing bodies have a statutory obligation to have regard to any representations made to them by the community, including parents.[26]

The rights of electors

Legislation provides for three types of "whistle blowers" who can call a halt to any illegal activities of a council or LEA.[27] An elector who is convinced that an LEA is about to act illegally can write to the monitoring officer at the council headquarters and ask for steps to be taken to halt the activity. An elector who is convinced that an LEA has incurred expenditure on promoting illegal activities can write to the chief financial officer at the council. If neither of these steps meets with success, the district auditor from the district audit service should be contacted. The address is in the telephone book. All three officers have a statutory duty to investigate complaints.

In the context of sex education, an elector might become convinced that an LEA was breaking the law by promoting homosexuality or encouraging schools to give sex education outside of the moral context required by the 1986 Act.

Contraceptive advice to the under 16s

In the Gillick case a mother of five daughters, all under the age of 16, objected to the giving of contraceptive advice or treatment to her daughters without her consent.[28] The law lords held that, whilst it would be most unusual, there were circumstances in which a doctor would be justified in giving such advice to a girl under 16 without the knowledge of her parents.

DES Circular 11/87 referred to the permissible circumstances of the Gillick judgement, stating that "these circumstances hinged essentially upon the nature and context of medical advice and treatment in connection with the supply and use of contraceptive devices. They have no parallel in school education".[29] The circular warned that for a teacher to give contraceptive advice to a pupil under the age of 16 "could, depending on the circumstances, amount to a criminal offence".[30]

During the preparation of circular 5/94, which replaced circular 11/87, the Department of Health and the sex education industry lobbied hard for a softer line.[31] The Family Planning Association claimed that teacher confidentiality was vitally important to 13 to 15 year olds.[32] However, the new guidance states that, as far as the duties of teachers are concerned, "giving an individual pupil advice on such matters without parental knowledge or consent would be an inappropriate exercise of a teacher's professional responsibilities. Teachers are not health professionals and the legal position of a teacher giving advice in such circumstances has never been tested in the Courts".[33]

The Gillick judgement remains and it is still worth quoting the advice which the government issued in 1987. Political pressure and not legal considerations have led to the weakening of guidance to schools.

Summary

The law has had to react to sex education which, in practice, has become increasingly explicit and amoral. Current legislation gives scope for determined and articulate parents to press their concerns. A group of parents acting in unison could exert considerable influence on a school or LEA. It is very important that parents' right to withdraw their children from sex education and the right to complain become well known.

Despite the law's insistence on a framework of family and moral values, there are far too many examples where this is simply ignored. The trend towards more explicit sex education will doubtless lead to calls for tougher regulation of the content of sex education, perhaps along the lines of American abstinence education which promotes chastity outside marriage and marital fidelity. A step in the right direction would be the consistent application of the 1986 Act's requirement that children are taught within a framework of family values.

Notes

1 The regulations were first made under Section 8 of the 1980 Education Act. The regulations were revoked under Statutory Instrument (SI) 1993/1502 but LEAs have a general duty to state their policies on the secular curriculum under Section 17 of the 1986 Education (No.2) Act.

2 The 1986 Education (No.2) Act, Section 18, and the Department for Education and Science (DES), Sex Education at School, Circular 11/87, para 9.

3 Circular 11/87 *op. cit.*, para 19.

4 *Loc. cit.*

5 *Ibid.*, para 22.

6 *Ibid.*, para 20.

7 Tingle, Rachel, *Gay Lessons: How public funds are used to promote Homosexuality among Children and Young People,* Pickwick Books, London, 1986.

8 *Ibid.*, p. 22.

9 The Education (national curriculum) Attainment Targets and Programmes of Study in Science, Order 1991: SI 1991/2897. See also *Science in the National Curriculum (1991)*, HMSO, London, 1991, p. 16.

10 See comments made in House of Lords Hansard, 11 June 1992, cols 1414-1466.

11 House of Lords Hansard, 11 June 1992 , cols 1414 -1466 (debate on a motion to amend the science order); 10 May 1993, col 1090 - 1119 (debate amendment to put teaching about sexual matters in the national curriculum under the remit of section 46 of the Education (No.2) Act 1986); 21 June 1993, col 119-142 (debate on an amendment to give a parental right of withdrawal the government announced it would bring forward its own amendments to meet Lord Stallard's concerns); 6 July

1993, cols 1290-1324 (debate on the government amendment which has become law).

12 The Education Act 1993, Section 241(4)(c).

13 The Education Act 1944, Section 114(1).

14 Department for Education (DFE), *The Education Act 1993: Sex Education in Schools*: Circular 5/94: para 17.

15 Circular 11/87 *op. cit.*, para 19.

16 Circular 5/94 *op. cit.*, para 8.

17 *Stonewall Postal Action Network (SPAN) Letter No 28*, 11 May 1993.

18 *The Guardian*, 7 December 1993.

19 Circular 5/94 *op. cit.*, annex A, page 19 - the guidance for Welsh schools is practically identical - see Welsh Office, *Sex Education in Schools*, Circular 45/94.

20 The Education Act 1993, Section 241(5)(b).

21 Education (School Information) (England) Regulations 1993, Schedule 2, para 9, SI 1993/1502.

22 Education (School Curriculum *etc.*) Regulations, Section 4A(b), SI 1989/954.

23 See Harris, N, *Complaints about Schooling*, The National Consumer Council, 1992.

24 1993 Education Reform Act, Schedule 6, para 7(2).

25 1988 Education Reform Act, Section 17A.

26 1986 Education Act, Section 18(3)(a).

27 The three officers are the monitoring officer (Local Government and Housing Act 1989, Section 5), the chief financial officer (Local Government Finance Act 1988, Section 114), and the district auditor (Local Government Finance Act 1982, Section 15).

28 *Gillick v. West Norfolk and Wisbech Area Health Authority and the Department of Health and Social Security* [1986] AC 112.

29 Circular 11/87 *op. cit.*, para 26.

30 *Loc. cit.*

31 See *The Times,* 7 May 1994.

32 See *The Independent*, 30 March 1994.

33 Circular 5/94 *op. cit.*, para 39.

4

Local Authority
Sex Education Policies

Paul Atkin

*Numbers in brackets, thus: (1), refer to sections of the
policy statements cited. These are listed at the end of
the chapter.*

Most parents want their children to have the safe and healthy type
of home life that is best provided by a two-parent family based on
marriage. Those who have read section 46 of the 1986 Education
(No.2) Act might therefore have been reassured to know that the
law requires authorities responsible for state-maintained schools to
ensure that sex education: "is given in such a manner as to
encourage those pupils to have due regard to moral considerations
and the value of family life". Furthermore, the Department for
Education's circular 5/94 gives some helpful examples of moral
considerations including "the importance of self restraint, dignity,
respect for themselves and others . . . loyalty and fidelity" (page 6).

While the circular recognises that many children do not come
from backgrounds which reflect such values, and sensitivity is
therefore needed to avoid causing hurt, teachers are nevertheless
encouraged "to help pupils, whatever their circumstances, to raise
their sights". However, classroom education takes place far from
Parliament and wise words in law are useless if they are not
implemented in the classroom.

This chapter examines local authorities' policies on sex education
because, while the task of implementing sex education programmes
ultimately falls to teachers and governing bodies, many schools are

51

guided by experts in county halls and regional councils. Most local education authorities (LEAs) produce sex education guidelines or policy statements which are revised in the light of changes in the law or, as this chapter will show, in spite of them.

Lip-service to the law

Circular 5/94 states that: "any LEA policy statement which refers to sex education is subject to section 46 of the 1986 Act" and many of the more recently-produced guidelines acknowledge this. Those for Bury, Lancashire, aim to promote an understanding of family life (3.1) and to foster a sense of moral responsibility in pupils (3.8), and the policy statement reproduces a school's legal obligations in full. By contrast, Lothian Regional Council's policy makes no reference to legal obligations and, although these guidelines were written before circular 5/94 reminded LEAs of their duties, Section 46 had been law for six years. The fact that the DFE found it necessary to re-emphasise the importance of this area in its circular suggests that Lothian was far from alone in its failure to acknowledge its obligations.

Many other LEA policies pay lip-service to family-centred sex education. There are brief mentions of the moral framework in introductory paragraphs or appendices but these are later contradicted by the main recommendations. Dorset, for example, recommends that pupils "examine sexual lifestyles" including celibacy, promiscuity and homosexuality (10). It is difficult to imagine how the latter two fit into a moral framework without inverting the very concept of morality itself - which is, as we shall see, exactly the outcome of LEA sex education.

Oxfordshire's policy refers to the 1986 Act, though not to section 46, and includes the suggestion that "a broad definition of sex education, incorporating all dimensions of sexuality and relationships, best serves the needs and rights of individuals and society" (3). An aim of this syllabus is "to counter . . . false assumptions of 'normal behaviour'" (14).

While Merton, London, refers prominently and frequently to the moral framework and insists that sex education teachers should have the competence to work within it, it is doubly disappointing that this important skill is blandly reduced to simply "exploring values and attitudes", discussing "opposing views" and promoting "respect for persons". The vital opportunity to explain the many benefits of faithful marriage and stable family life is lost.

Semantic gymnastics

All sex education guidelines studied were implicitly hostile to the view that the two-parent family based on marriage was the best possible place for children to grow and develop. Writers of many LEA syllabuses go to imaginative and often ridiculous lengths to avoid references to traditional family life.

Although 72% of children live with their two married parents and only 1% live with neither,[1] some sex educators appear to be writing for a generation of orphans and go to great lengths to avoid the word parent. For example; the still influential guidelines from the National Curriculum Council describe children as living with "important adults" (14) while 5 year olds in Sheffield live with "special people".

Similarly, most guidelines relegate the nuclear family to one option among many "different types of family", giving the impression that it does not matter if you have one parent or two. This defies both common sense and all the evidence which shows that the real family has no equivalent.[2] Despite this, many LEAs begin relationship reductionism early, between the ages of five and seven, when it is difficult for children to cope with any implied criticism of their home arrangements.

Marriage is another taboo. Despite the fact that most children will grow up to marry, Dorset regards it more important to teach them about "loving and caring relationships", not mentioning the responsibilities and commitment of marriage until the pupils are about 15. Oxfordshire, too, regards "intimacy in loving and caring relationships" as a foundation of its sex education programme. Marriage is referred to as a ritual (18) and otherwise only spoken of in the context of divorce (24). Norfolk children are given relationship education throughout their school lives covering assertiveness, self-abuse and safer sex in Key Stages 1 to 3 and only going on to learn about "marriage, divorce, separation", at Key Stage 4. Lothian regards marriage as one of a number of types of relationship whilst Merton suggest that pupils brainstorm their way through various forms of sexual relationship including "one night stands and established relationships" but not married love, wherein sexual expression is still most commonly found.

A moral vacuum

For the principles of right and wrong, policy-makers substitute choices, decisions and risks, occasionally good and bad, and even irresponsible but almost never right or wrong. The definition of morality is thereby inverted; no longer is it a universal code of behaviour accepted because it is the most beneficial to society, rather it becomes a matter of subjective personal decision with little regard for wider consequences. Oxfordshire is the most explicit. Morals and morality are classified as "sensitive issues" so that "We cannot force or oblige children to 'be good'. People develop their own morality; they test their core values and beliefs against their experience. By this process they develop, own and implement their personal moral code" (33).

In Oxfordshire, sex education is "an umbrella term of all the learning we need in order to understand our own and others' sexuality and to develop skills for relationships and informed decision making" (6). Unsurprisingly, therefore, while bisexuality, homosexuality, fetishism, lesbianism, masturbation and pornography all feature in Oxfordshire's *abc of sex education*, chastity, fidelity, right and wrong do not. North Yorkshire also adopts a sexual shopping list for pupils from age 11, who are expected to cover topics such as self-gratification, auto-eroticism, making and breaking relationships and the value of sexual expression in relationships (15/16). This last topic makes a judgement which demonstrates an approving attitude towards teenage sex and which, if practised at the age from which it is taught, would be illegal. Typical of LEA guidelines, North Yorkshire's secondary school programme is no more than a set of technical instructions in a moral void. Likewise

Kirklees, Yorkshire, focuses on the pupils' personal attitudes, beliefs, feelings and experiences (7.5.2). Teachers, we are told, are not "experts with an authoritative view" but "facilitators".

No LEA policy that we have seen gives clear guidance on sexual behaviour and all are steeped in individualistic morality. Only Merton refers to respect for truth and the difference between right and wrong (11), but again these concepts are undermined by the suggestion that they could be set in the context of an equal opportunities policy "within which each individual and their circumstances are valued" (11) including, presumably, the promiscuous and the perverse.

In Dorset it is recommended that the AIDS programme include "discussion of ways of avoiding health risks posed by certain forms of sexual behaviour" (14). It would surely be more practicable, as well as moral, simply to tell pupils not to indulge in the homosexual behaviour to which this refers. Both Merton's and Dorset's policies include a directory of local sexually-transmitted disease clinics; no doubt for those who fall victim to their ambiguous advice.

Feminist brainwashing

Many LEAs' policies try to counter what they regard as sexual stereotyping, such as girls playing house and boys playing soldiers. This quest for androgyny starts early in Dorset where 5-7 year olds learn to "develop skills to counter media and other pressures to conform to sex stereotyping"(7), while older pupils are encouraged to consider "the effect of gender roles and stereotyping on sexual behaviour". This suggestion, that men and women are attracted to each other because of societal pressure, would be ridiculous if it were not an implicit invitation to consider homosexuality as a legitimate way of life. Oxfordshire also takes up this improbable suggestion with the speculative idea that "labelling and stereotyping can have a negative effect on mental health" (22).

As part of its equal opportunities policy, Kirklees recommends that all pupils should be exposed to "positive" role-models. In practice the equality industry might use this term to denote anything from female paratroopers to male nannies but never to the "conventionally limiting" three roles: mother, father, husband or wife.[3] What is normal is ignored or portrayed as negative whilst the odd, unusual and unlikely are held up as something to aspire to. It seems likely that the most damage to mental health would be among those children exposed to these unnatural and confusing ideas.

Sensitive issues

All sex education programmes feature sensitive issues and most reflect their authors' beliefs that contraception is desirable and homosexuality morally neutral, that AIDS affects all sectors of the population equally, and that abortion is exclusively a matter of women's rights.

Eight year olds in Sheffield are educated about condoms and, at 11, they are told about the coil, the pill and where to go for confidential advice. The Brook Advisory Centre once put a 10 year old on the pill[4] so Sheffield recommends their contraceptive display-pack as a useful resource for children of this age. Oxfordshire introduces family planning from age 11 to allow "young people to learn to *talk* easily about contraception long before they need to use it" (22). Despite its prefatory emphasis on the moral framework, Merton suggests that secondary school pupils should receive practical demonstrations of the correct use of male and female condoms (40). Lothian paradoxically describes contraception as an aspect of human reproduction (11).

Section 28 of the Local Government Act 1988 prevents schools from promoting homosexuality as a type of family relationship and most authorities refer to this in their guidelines, though such references are usually followed by a note that the "objective discussion" of homosexuality is permissible. In the moral void which sex education promotes, homosexuality is presented as merely one of several types of sexual behaviour which, like everything else, is a matter of individual choice. Merton recommends, as a guiding principle, that curriculum content should include "exploration of sexuality" and "respect for various sexual orientations"(14). Oxfordshire aims to encourage "unembarrassed acceptance of sexuality" while Norfolk recommends that 11 to 14 year olds should have "an awareness of the range of human sexuality, heterosexuality, homosexuality, being lesbian and bisexuality" (21). These statements are a green light for anyone who wishes to take the gay agenda into schools and conveniently ignore the fact that two authoritative studies have recently demonstrated that homosexual behaviour is so rare that there is no genuine reason to include it in school programmes.[5] The use of sex education as vehicle for homosexual proselytising needs to be urgently examined.

How do they do that?

Many sex education methods are very different from those of traditional teaching. Most programmes recommend "active learning methods" such as role-play and group-discussion. Although presented as the free exchange of ideas, group discussion is simply another form of instruction disguised as "choice" and training experts acknowledge that it is a very effective way of modifying attitudes.[6] During sex education, therefore, this public discussion of private matters is used to break down individual reservations and produce significantly more liberal attitudes.

At the school level, many guidelines suggest a cross-curricular or whole-school approach, which brings sex education into many other subjects. For sex educators this is a useful way of reaching all pupils because, while parents may withdraw their children from designated sex education lessons, they will still be exposed to the programmes in other lessons. Many courses also recommend a "spiral curriculum" so that issues covered are reinforced by repetition.

Religious sex education

Many British schools are formally affiliated to religious denominations whose ethics permeate the curriculum. The largest group of such schools are run by the Catholic church, whose teachings firmly support authentic family life. Official Catholic bodies have given their schools sex education guidance which is likely to have more impact than that produced by the local LEA. Regrettably, in the same way as many LEAs pay little attention to the law, Catholic educational organisations fail to observe, or even oppose, their church's teaching on sexuality.

In Scotland, the Archdiocese of St. Andrews and Edinburgh's education pack, *HIV Prevention - A Christian Response*, was written by the Rev. Tom Williams, a Catholic priest, and Rhona Hutchinson, a community education worker and apparently a former client of the Brook Advisory Centre. Not surprisingly, the pack shows the influence of Brook throughout.

In particular, children play 'The Options Game', in which they are dealt playing cards listing activities which may lead to HIV contamination. The children are instructed to categorise these as "safe", "not safe" or "don't know" and discussion follows. The same exercise (now known as 'The Risk Game') occurs in a similar pack, produced by the Brook Advisory Centre, which specialises in giving contraceptives to children without their parents' knowledge. The aims of this game are:

- To enable participants to become aware of a wide range of sexual practices and their feelings about them
- To help participants develop the ability to speak openly and explicitly about sexual behaviour (41).

Although the stated aims of the two 'games' are different, the content is remarkably similar and it is therefore reasonable to expect the same outcomes, most fully stated above by Brook. This table compares some of the discussion topics in the two games:

ARCHDIOCESE OF ST ANDREWS & EDINBURGH	BROOK ADVISORY CENTRE
The Options Game	*The Risk Game*
Sleeping with someone who has AIDS	Sleeping with someone who has AIDS
Having sexual contact which stops short of intercourse	Having sexual contact which stops short of intercourse

Having a heavy petting session	Having a heavy petting session
Having a man-to-man physical relationship (homosexual sex)	Having a man-to-man physical relationship (homosexual sex)
Having sex when drunk	Having sex when drunk
Having casual sex abroad	Having casual sex abroad
Having vagina sex if you are on the Pill	Having vagina sex if you are on the Pill
Having sex with your husband/wife/partner	Having sex with your husband/wife/partner
Having lots of different sexual partners	Having lots of different sexual partners
Having anal sex	Having anal sex
Having anal sex using a condom	Having anal sex using a condom
Using the withdrawal method (the man withdrawing his penis before ejaculation)	Using the withdrawal method (the man withdrawing his penis before ejaculation)

Whether the Catholic church in Edinburgh is using material written by Brook or *vice versa* will matter less to Catholic parents than that their children will be working through this sexual encyclopaedia.

Although all forms of contraception and homosexual activity are against Catholic teaching, *HIV Prevention - A Christian Response* also includes practical hints on the advantages and disadvantages of condoms and abstinence. The stated disadvantage of the latter is that it is "challenging" (Factsheet Four). Similarly, Judith Bury, a long time director of Brook contributes a long article on 'Teenage Sexual Behaviour and the impact of AIDS' which includes a discussion of teenage homosexual behaviour and the use of contraception. Authors Williams and Hutchinson fail to mention

Bury's involvement with Brook and describe her only as a worker with the local health board.

HIV Prevention - A Christian Response goes against Catholic teaching, yet it has received the *imprimatur* - a Catholic quality assurance mark certifying it free from doctrinal or moral error - from Archbishop Keith Patrick O'Brien of St Andrews and Edinburgh.

Regrettably, *HIV Prevention - A Christian Response* is no isolated example. In 1994 the Catholic Education Service, an agency of the English and Welsh bishops' conference, sent a copy of their newly-published *Education in Sexuality* to every Catholic school. As source-materials, the book recommends *Knowing Me Knowing You* for primary schools and *Taught not Caught* for secondary pupils. *Knowing Me Knowing You* includes a quiz in which children must answer true or false to (among others) the following statements:

- For sexual penetration to take place a man's penis has to be hard;
- For sexual penetration to take place a condom has to be worn;
- A climax for a man is when sperm comes out of his body;
- People are noisy when they have sexual intercourse.

It also describes condoms and caps, and incorrectly suggests that natural birth regulation, the only method approved by the church, is ineffective.[7]

Taught not Caught was written by an Australian feminist collective and is recommended by the UK Family Planning Association. One session for 16 year olds which aims "to increase tolerance towards a range of expressions of sexuality" includes a discussion of the following situations:

- Parents are in bed together having sexual intercourse when their three year old enters the room. They include the child in their embrace.
- A mother is changing her baby son's nappy. He shows by giggling that he enjoys having his penis touched. She continues to touch him all over, including his penis.
- A boy sits on his grandfather's knee. Grandfather strokes his hair.[8]

Conclusions

Sex education is the product of the abortion and birth control lobbies; it exists to transmit their ideology to school children. It is therefore not surprising that its content often varies between the ambiguous and the obscene. Despite the clear legal direction that such education must be given in the context of family life and with due regard to moral considerations, LEAs are largely implementing a value-free agenda with only the occasional nods towards genuine family life and objective morality. Although the latest government guidance clearly restates the obligation to respect family life, LEA policies produced since its publication show no greater inclination to do so and, in practice, continue to present such life as no more than one option among many.

LEA sex education policies are public documents and, in addition, every school is required to have a written sex education policy which is likely to be based on their content. This policy must be available for inspection. It is the right and duty of parents to find out what their children are being taught and vigorously to demand that the law is obeyed.

Sources: Guidelines and Policy Statements

Archdiocese of St Andrews and Edinburgh, *HIV Prevention - A Christian Response*, Rev Tom Williams and Rhona Hutchinson, 1993

Catholic Education Service, *Education in Sexuality. Some Guidelines for Teachers and Governors in Catholic Schools*, 1994

Department for Education, Education Act 1993: Sex Education in Schools, Circular number 5/94, 6 May 1994

Dorset Education Authority, Dorset Curriculum Guidelines No. 2 - *Sex Education*, February 1991

Kirklees Education Service, *Personal and Social Education from 5 to 19 - Guidelines for Schools and Colleges*, 13 February 1990

Lothian Regional Council Education Department, *Health Education. A Statement of Policy for Nursery, Primary and Secondary Stages of Education*, 1993

Metropolitan Borough of Bury, *Sex Education in Schools - L.E.A. Policy Statement,* August 1994

Merton Curriculum & Assessment Unit and Merton, Sutton & Wandsworth Health Promotion Unit, *Sex Education Guidelines*, June 1994

National Curriculum Council, Curriculum Guidance 5, *Health Education*, 1990

Norfolk County Council Education Department, *Sex Education Guidelines for Teachers and Staff in Schools*, May 1992

North Yorkshire County Council Education Department, *Sex Education Guidelines*, July 1992

Oxfordshire Education Service, *Oxfordshire Curriculum Matters 9, Sex Education, Teaching & Learning About Sexuality and Relationships*, July 1992

Sheffield Education Authority, *Guidelines for Sex Education*, summer 1992

Burns, Jo, and Wright, Cathie, *A Trainer's Guide to Workshops on Young People and Sexuality in the Context of HIV/AIDS*, Brook Advisory Centre, Workers' Educational Association, Lothian Health Department, HMSO, 1993

Notes

1   Robert Whelan, *Broken Homes and Battered Children*, Family Education Trust, 1994, p. 21.

2   Norman Dennis and George Erdos, *Families Without Fatherhood*, IEA Health and Welfare Unit, second edition, 1993; Jon Davies (Ed.), *The Family: is it just another lifestyle choice?* IEA Health and Welfare Unit, 1993; Robert Whelan, *op. cit.*

3 Equal Opportunities Commission, *An Equal Start*, 1994, p. 13.

4 'The girl of 10 they put on the pill', *Daily Mail*, 5 November 1983; 'On the pill at 10', *Daily Star*, 5 November 1983.

5 Kaye Wellings *et al.*, *Sexual Behaviour in Britain*, Penguin, 1994; Robert T. Michael *et al.*, *Sex in America - A Definitive Survey*, Little, Brown and Company, 1994.

6 Margaret Reid, Harry Barrington and John Kenney, *Training Interventions*, Institute of Personnel Management, 1992, p. 96.

7 Thomas Regan, 'Vigilance is Vital', *Catholic Times*, 16 October 1994.

8 Valerie Riches, *Sex and Social Engineering*, Family Education Trust, 1986, p. 21.

5

AIDS: A Suitable Case for Treatment?

Patricia Morgan

When AIDS first appeared in the early 1980s it was treated as a major public health problem. In America there was talk of a devastating rise in heterosexual cases.[1] In Britain there were warnings that soon almost every family would be affected by the AIDS problem and that society might collapse.[2]

Gone was the boast that modern antibiotics had seen off "God's little allies" – the old sexually transmitted diseases – which permissives like Alex Comfort saw as a prop of traditional "moralistic direction".[3] Some warned that people would persecute the victims: "A dark but predictable side of human nature is that any mysterious epidemic will give rise to scapegoating".[4]

A disease like no other?

Given the initial scare, it is hardly surprising that tremendous attention was given to HIV/AIDS. By 1992 around 36,000 scientific papers had been published on the subject and no other area of medicine received so much resource.[5] British Regional Health Authorities (RHAs) spent tens of times more on each AIDS patient, and thousands of times more on each AIDS death than on, for example, people with heart disease. By 1994/5 the total amount available to spend on any AIDS related work reached £214 million. Mersey RHA spent £305,263 per live case in 1991/2. However, "at a time of financial stringency in the public services and especially when many claim that the NHS is underfunded",[6] most RHAs underspent their AIDS budgets, even though they tried hard to get rid of the money through "schemes inviting ridicule".[7]

AIDS also provided unprecedented levels of employment in medical and non-medical fields – about as many full-time workers as people with the disease, not including people in local authorities, charities, research councils and industry. In Orkney and the Outer Hebrides, with no HIV or AIDS, there were three workers spending a ring-fenced budget of £70,000 in 1992.

This HIV/AIDS sector of public employment has a " . . . mind boggling proliferation of 'jobs' such as safe-sex advisors, condom project workers, HIV liaison workers, AIDS ethnic outreach workers, local AIDS health co-ordinators. Prefix 'AIDS' or 'HIV' to 'co-ordinator', 'liaison officer', 'worker' and link this to an area of welfare provision such as children, teenagers, women, IUDs, ethnic minorities, prisons, the deaf, disabled, *etc.*, and you have a £17,000 to £20,000 job. The big growth this year [1991/2] is safe sex education in schools, where the bureaucracy want to provide for kids as young as eight years old".[8]

Many full-time personnel have no professional qualifications and are often employed by organisations not subject to formal audit. Many are engaged in an educational campaign which "assumes that all of the sexually active population and infants of all mothers are potentially or actually at risk".[9] The Health Education Authority lists 265 educational "resources" and 212 HIV/AIDS helplines. If we add counselling services, information networks, HIV units and so forth, there is about one AIDS organisation for every three sufferers.

The services and materials produced by these AIDS bodies often cater for schools. While Section 241 of the 1993 Education Act requires secondary schools to provide sex education, the "law does not define the purpose or content of sex education, other than declaring that it includes education about HIV and AIDS and other sexually transmitted diseases".[10]

The epidemic that never was?

It might be argued that the scale of the AIDS problem could justify at least some of the attention paid to it (and money spent). However, despite the doomsday scenario, there is no AIDS epidemic in any developed country. In Britain, from the time AIDS first appeared till mid-1994, 6,388 people died from it while 2.5 million died of cardiovascular diseases. The AIDS death figures are probably inflated by diseases like Kaposi's sarcoma which can accompany AIDS or HIV infection but are not necessarily caused by HIV.

AIDS is often portrayed as affecting all sectors of the population yet, if one looks at AIDS deaths in terms of transmission, three quarters involve sexual intercourse between men in the developed world. Statistics to mid-1994 suggest that, of the 3,524 reports of HIV infection through heterosexual acts, 74% had had a sexual partner from a country, invariably in Africa, where heterosexual transmission was usual. There have been only 96 cases where the sexual partner has come from the UK and is not identifiable as a bisexual, drug user or haemophiliac. Even of the 37,000 AIDS victims in New York city, only 69 cases up to 1992 seemed to have been transmitted heterosexually without other identifiable risks. Caution is still necessary, however, since detailed investigation of samples of those supposedly infected through heterosexual intercourse have revealed other risk factors in many of the cases.[11]

AIDS offers virtually no threat to women or children. From 1981 to 1991, there were only nine deaths of women not in a high risk category in the UK.[12] Extensive research among London prostitutes reported in 1993 that only two were HIV positive; both injected drugs. It was estimated that about five prostitutes in Britain might have the virus.[13]

To the end of April 1994 there had been 544 reports of HIV infected children aged 14 or less in the UK, and a total of 163 AIDS cases in children, of whom 87 are known to have died. If the children were not infected through contaminated blood, then it was through transmission from the mother before or during birth, or from breast milk. Those involved are often recent arrivals from Africa.

Figures showing increases in heterosexual transmission invariably involve imported cases. The AIDS bureaucracy has played on unusual instances of HIV among women in London while concealing the fact that these relate to HIV contracted in Africa.

Because people are infected abroad does not mean that there is an epidemic in this country, or that there ever will be.

Similarly, because AIDS spreads heterosexually in Africa, it does not follow that it will here. Moreover, HIV data from Africa "are largely uninvalidated, differently distributed in demographic and geographic terms, overlap to an unknown extent with infections which are uncommon or non-existent in Britain and related to risks and life styles which are totally different".[14]   As Stewart, Craven and Taghavi conclude, the HIV risk to anyone outside high-risk groups is "negligible".[15]

Despite these facts, fantasy has run riot. There were no women with AIDS over 40 in the country when Sheila Gilchrist, Positively Women's director, argued: "There is no pattern emerging: there is no group that is more at risk than any other".[16] AIDS sufferers in Oxfordshire were few yet its health authority's epidemiologist declared that "there is no doubt that the heterosexual epidemic has begun . . . It is affecting anyone who is sexually active".[17]

The sex explosion

Not only has AIDS been paid a disproportionate amount of attention, but AIDS education is a main reason why children have been exposed to so much sex at so early an age, from so many directions – both in schools and the world around them.

In Sheffield eight year olds can be told how people get AIDS, why they need condoms and to think whether their Mum or Dad has AIDS. At 12, pupils must recognise "the right to have sex with the partner of one's choice". At 13, we move on to "the pleasure of having sex with the partner of your choice". The important thing is "freedom to choose what you feel happy and comfortable with doing" and places to go for "confidential" help if parents interfere. At age 14 there are "safety measures in dealing with accidental spillage of body fluids". Marriage, "family lifestyles" (*sic*) and parenthood are mentioned so that pupils can be told that there are "other valid choices".

One boy described how a lady from a hospital AIDS department came to his classroom and wrote obscenities on the blackboard. She told the mixed class of teenagers that many heterosexual couples had anal sex, and that 50% of local youngsters were already "sexually active" by 16 (national figures are that 27% of boys and 17% of girls aged 16-24 had first intercourse before 16).[18]

Not long ago, it was adults' responsibility to order and regulate adolescence and steer young people through this special stage of life. As Barbara Dafoe Whitehead observes,[19] this involved a moratorium on youth sexual activity, which provided the opportunities for youngsters to acquire the competence and qualifications for adulthood. Now adults must provide juveniles with the tools to access, express and manage their sexuality as a normal part of growing up.

According to the AIDS Education and Research Trust (AVERT), people move from one casual coupling to another. The trust tells youngsters that few people have "only one sexual partner in their lives" anyway, so they must keep their condoms handy since, "as you get older the more uncertainty there will be about a new partner's sexual history". Moreover, "Many young people go on holiday either abroad or in this country to meet people and have a good time. Sex can be part of the fun. So if you think you may be sexually active take condoms with you".[20]

In Australia vans from the AIDS bureau " . . . promote safe sex to children on the beach. They were also giving out free condoms and, if you picked one with a star on it, you got a T-shirt".[21]

Permissive parental values – reinforced by AIDS education – and low parental monitoring predispose children to early sexual activity, and adolescents who perceive their parents as accepting early sexual activity are more likely to be sexually experienced.[22]

In the post-AIDS perspective we are expected to reject notions of abnormality or deviancy, or measures of normality and morality. The only rule is to use contraception. In Jon Davies' words: "There is . . . no sexual ethic, no sexual system, no evaluation of sexual acts in terms of extrinsic purpose . . . and therefore . . . there is no call to surround sexual activity with any rules other than the day-to-day rules of advertising and *caveat emptor*, such as appear for example in the Sausage Rolls and Meat Pie Regulations (1976) or health warnings on cigarette packets".[23]

Television similarly witnesses to a "society which endlessly sniggers and is consumed by smut".[24]

Liberation complete?

The full acceptance of homosexual practice is seen as an important part of the way to further the sexual revolution. A BBC Radio 4 St Valentine's Day celebration of homosexuality "contrived to give the impression that the frolicsome cheering body . . . were . . . the harbingers of a new age, pointing the way from the bondage of ancient prejudice toward a golden future of universal emancipation".[25]

Homosexual campaigners form a politically influential group which "explicitly challenges the legitimacy of a heterosexual establishment and increasingly seeks confrontation with it".[26] The gay counter-culture, where the individual is "the centre of my own world", can be recruited to undermine "the one institution that has served mankind since the dawn of history . . . the basic cell upon which every known civilisation has been built".[27] Homosexuality is the ultimate challenge and final solution to the family.

In fact, the move is to reduce heterosexuality to the same genital imperatives as homosexuality. "Homosexuality is not the attraction of opposites which demands careful negotiation for success, but like unto like. The requirements on the male to come to terms with the demands of female emotion, by learning to respond in kind is absent. No painful self-adjustment is necessary; no personal growth results".[28]

The pivotal role of homosexuality in the sexual revolution means that AIDS victims are portrayed as martyrs for love, or sacrificial victims of an oppressive society.[29] Since AIDS has been invested with such ideological significance, it is hard to deal with it on a par with other diseases. AIDS has national days when people wear red ribbons to commemorate the fallen. Some wear pink ribbons, just for the gay victims. There are no yellow ribbons for lung cancer, or green ones for multiple sclerosis.

Getting control

The emergence of AIDS as a major public health issue in the 1980s " . . . represents an extreme example of the way in which the concerns of minority groups . . . can demand and obtain disproportionate allocations of public resources by the use of political pressure".[30]

The national AIDS educational campaign is based on an epidemic model of disease, yet such a model "is not valid because the main risks arise from certain types of sexual behaviour, consumption of drugs and blood transfusion". Public policy towards AIDS can only be justified if HIV is easily transmitted, "which it is not".[31] As David Rogers of American National Commission on AIDS admitted in 1991, AIDS "was not a communicable disease in the classical sense. The only merciful thing about AIDS is that it is so hard to catch".[32]

Instead, it is "obvious from the distribution of AIDS in Britain and the United States that life style and personal behaviour are major determinants of the original and continuing incidence". Thus: "It follows that health education should be directed at high risk groups and should concentrate upon the avoidance of high risk behaviour".[33]

The Facts about HIV and AIDS, the Health Education Authority's pamphlet, while stating that anal sex carries a high risk, also claims that unprotected vaginal sex "also carries a high risk". This is potentially misleading. Indeed, in its own more up-market *Health Update 4: Sexual Health*, the HEA states how: "Clearly, thus far cases of AIDS and deaths from AIDS have been concentrated among men who have sex with men".[34] Few women are HIV positive "because the major route of transmission is sex between men".[35]

In its *HIV & AIDS; A Guide for Journalists*, the HEA claims that: "Although gay men, injecting drug users and haemophiliacs have been disproportionately affected in the United Kingdom, it is misleading and dangerous to talk about high risk groups".[36] Instead, a "more relevant term is 'high risk behaviour'".

Not only are children among the lowest risk groups for HIV, but no amount of sexually explicit education explaining the practicalities of anal intercourse, or drama workshops in which to "explore" the important "issues and dilemmas" of AIDS,[37] could have helped those who have become infected.

It can be argued that " . . . the foisting of condoms on children, the effort to accustom them to their use, the treatment of condoms generally that bordered on the ancient Roman worship of phalluses, is difficult to construe as anything less than decadent. One need not be a certified moralist, a conservative, or a Christian to be horrified at what the condomites passed off as responsible behaviour in time of crisis".[38]

While the HEA admits that "There are still a relatively small number of heterosexual people infected. However, we do not know the true number of infected people (because not everyone has been tested) and the numbers are growing".[39]

Another way to spread the risks around is to insist that practices like anal intercourse are far more usual than people like to admit and that homosexuals form a large percentage of the population. Yet, a large-scale University of Chicago survey showed in 1994, only 2.7% of men admitted to a homosexual experience in the past year.[40] The vast majority (96%) of the population preferred conventional vaginal intercourse and 81% of women had not tried anything else. Findings echo those from Britain, showing how homosexuality and promiscuity are far less widespread than asserted by the AIDS campaigners.[41]

Perhaps, as the government says, "From the word go, we took HIV and AIDS very seriously. That is why we have a lower prevalence rate than other countries".[42] It is, however, difficult to prove the succcess of a campaign against something that might not have happened anyway.

The safe option?

The AIDS industry has been a "major policy error" with "a substantial misallocation of resources for the funding of proposed, current and recent past publicity . . . "[43] As Michael Fumento remarks: "persons who tried to be specific about the mode of infection would be accused of being insensitive and hateful".[44] The AIDS establishment was "at complete loggerheads with the entire purpose of the science of epidemiology, which is to identify where a disease is occurring and how it is spreading in order to reduce its incidence".[45]

As the disease became fashionable, the AIDS establishment consolidated. With the abolition of the GLC and spending constraints on local authorities, activists could board the AIDS gravy train by migrating to the centrally funded 'voluntary' sector.[46]

In 1991, AIDS education for 11 to 14 year olds was made a compulsory part of the science course in the National Curriculum. There was no consultation and it was not in the original draft.[47] Not only did parents have no right to withdraw a child from lessons, but local authorities were given the right to prosecute schools or parents who failed to co-operate with their teaching.

However, the 1986 Education Act had required that governors ensure that sex education "is given in such a manner as to encourage those pupils to have due regard to moral considerations and the value of family life". Critics made it clear that they saw this as the way that the Thatcher government had "given way to the moral right" (Giles Radice, Labour's education spokesman). "We must all", Ian McKellan told a rally against the Act "be out and about, in the streets, in the classrooms . . . promoting homosexuality".[48]

In the face of protest, AIDS education was dropped from the overloaded science curriculum to reappear as a requirement in sex education. The National Foundation for Educational Research's survey of parents' views on sex education,[49] found that more than 70% of parents would not consider withdrawal from sex education at all, although homosexuality was the main topic which parents indicated that they might want their children to avoid.

Missing the risks

AIDS education is a feast of misinformation. It not only trades on risks which are minimal or non-existent but also underwrites risk-taking behaviour, by suggesting that homosexual practices are normal and usual. AVERT's booklet *AIDS & Sex Information for Young People* does not mention that anal intercourse is any more risky than vaginal.

The Sigma research into the sexual behaviour of homosexual and bisexual men actually reports that more men were having anal sex and having it with more partners " . . . than were at the start of the study [1987]: this may be a sign that they are more comfortable with sex and less afraid of the risks of sex. This has coincided with the more pro-sex stance of safer sex campaigns aimed at gay men".[50]

Foremost in the field of sex/AIDS education and with a massive budget is the Terrence Higgins Trust - an organisation run by homosexual activists for active homosexuals. Their output is highly pornographic and appears to meet the conditions for official funding and recommendation because the text refers to condoms at certain points.

AIDS education as sexual propaganda provides a resource for those appointed by local authorities to give encouragement and support to youngsters to develop a homosexual identity out of what may only be a passing phase. AIDS educators are also very keen to disabuse anyone of notions that restrictions on sexual partners or delaying sexual experience have any prophylactic effect, compared to the mighty condom.[51]

A guide to services for the handicapped from the London Borough of Hounslow dismisses "being faithful" and insists instead how: "It is more effective to practise safer sex every time than to cut down on sexual partners".[52]

However, in its *Health Update 4: Sexual Health*,[53] the HEA itself casts doubt upon all the assertions it makes elsewhere about the cast-iron protection provided by condoms: " . . . condoms reduce the risk of HIV transmission rather than prevent it". Unsurprisingly, awareness of HIV/AIDS among young people is not matched by knowledge of the STDs they are far more likely to catch.[54] While STDs are overwhelmingly concentrated among adolescent girls and young women aged 15-24, "awareness of their impact on the health of infected women has not increased proportionately".[55]

Similarly "the present focus on contraception and safe sex fails to address the way that problems of STDs and unintended teenage pregnancy are associated with greater sexual involvement by ever younger teenagers. Again, what ought to be tackled is 'primary problematic behaviour'".[56] A Swiss program focusing on safe sex and not on postponing intercourse led to a doubling of the number of 16 year old girls having intercourse.[57]

Much evidence is that early sex is exploitative, if not downright coercive, for a large proportion of under 16s, let alone the 10 to 14 year olds. While the emphasis is now on giving children positive messages about sex, we seldom hear about the advantages of avoiding sex until you are emotionally, mentally and physically grown up.

It is time to dismantle the whole complex of vested interests, bureaucracy and circus that has accumulated around AIDS. Funding for the AIDS industry must be brought into proportion with the numbers infected, who should be treated on the same basis as sufferers from any other serious disease. The present approach only degrades sexuality and serves the ends of special interest groups for whom the welfare of children is low on the agenda.

Notes

1   Charles Bremner, 'The fruit of the Age of Aquarius is the new age of puritanism', *The Times*, 7 February 1987.

2   Susil Gupta, 'The AIDS Fraud', *Analysis*, winter 1991/2, pp. 22-44, quoting from Dr Devlin in *She* magazine, September 1985, and *The Guardian*, 29 November 1990.

3   Alex Comfort, *The Anxiety Makers*, Panther, 1968, p. 197.

4   Micheal Fumento, *The Myth of Heterosexual AIDS*, Regnery Gateway, 1990.

5   B.M.Craven, G.T.Stewart and M.Taghavi 'Amateurs Confronting Specialists: Expenditure on AIDS in England', *Journal of Public Policy*, Vol. 13, 1993, pp. 305-325, p. 305.

6 *Ibid.*, p. 312.

7 *Ibid.*, p. 314.

8 Susil Gupta, *op. cit.*, p. 41.

9 B.M.Craven, G.T.Stewart and M.Taghavi, *op.cit.*, p. 314.

10 Education Act 1993: Sex Education in Schools Circular number 5/94, DFE, p. 7.

11 See B.M.Craven, G.T.Stewart and M.Taghavi, *op. cit.*; also PHLS CDSC 'AIDS and HIV infection in the United Kingdom; monthly report', *Communicable Disease Report*, 4 (28), 1994, pp. 131-134; and *Health Update 4: Sexual Health*, HEA, 1994.

12 V.L.Gilbert *et al.*, 'Second generation heterosexual transmission of HIV-1 infection', *CDR Review*, Vol. 2, No. 5, 24 April 1992.

13 Nick Nuttal 'Hospital finds HIV ratc low in prostitutes', *The Times* (referring to the *British Medical Journal*), 6 August 1993.

14 Susil Gupta *op.cit.*, p. 34.

15 Gordon Stewart, Barrie Craven and Majid Taghavi, *op. cit.*

16 Susil Gupta (quoting from *Triple Jeapody: Women and AIDS*, The Panos Institute, 1990), *op. cit.*, p. 31.

17 Susil Gupta (quoting 'Concern in Shires over Heterosexual AIDS Cases', *Daily Telegraph*, 20 September 1991), *op. cit.*, p. 23.

18 A.M.Johnson *et al.*, *Sexual Attitudes and Lifestyles*, Blackwell Scientific Publications, 1994.

19 Barbara Dafoe Whitehead, 'The Failure of Sex Education', *Atlantic Monthly*, October 1994.

20 *AIDS & Sex Information for Young People*, AVERT, The AIDS Education and Research Trust, 1994.

21 Jane Wheatley, 'Putting the rough-sea riders under Raps', *The Times Saturday Review*, 6 February 1993.

22 Stephen A.Small and Tom Luster, 'Adolescent Sexual Activity: An Ecological, Risk Factor Approach', *Journal of Marriage and the Family* 56, February 1994, pp. 181-192.

23 Jon Davies, 'From Household to Family to Individualism' in Jon Davies (Ed.), *The Family: Is it just another lifestyle choice?*, IEA Health and Welfare Unit, Choice in Welfare, No. 15, 1993.

24 Henry Porter, 'A vulgar little screen', *The Daily Telegraph*, 14 January 1995; Ryan Gilbey, 'Sexy. But think again about the Y-fronts', *The Independent*, 13 January 1995.

25 E.J.Mishan, 'What's Gay About Homosexuality?', *The Salisbury Review*, September 1993.

26 *Ibid.*

27 E.J.Mishan, *op. cit.*

28 Clifford Longley, 'Christianity must speak now on sexual imperatives', *The Daily Telegraph*, 2 December 1994.

29 Joan Acocella 'Dancer with a black rage against his own dying light', *Financial Times*, 9 January 1995.

30 Robert Whelan, 'The AIDS scandal', *Economic Affairs*, June 1991.

31 B.M.Craven, G.T.Stewart and M.Taghavi, *op. cit.*, p. 310.

32 Quoted by Susil Gupta, *op. cit.,* p. 42.

33 B.M.Craven, G.T.Stewart and M Taghavi, *op. cit.*, p. 310.

34 *Health Update 4: Sexual Health*, Health Education Council, 1994, p.7.

35 *Health Update 4: Sexual Health (op. cit.)*, p. 9.

36 *HIV & AIDS; A Guide for Journalists*, Health Education Authority.

37 See, *e.g.*, Pete Saunders and Clare Farquhar, *Positively Primary: Strategies for Approaching HIV/AIDS with Primary School Children*, AVERT, 1994.

38 Micheal Fumento, *op. cit.*, p. 177.

39 *Talking to TEENAGERS about AIDS, op. cit.*

40 Report by Christine Hardyment, 'Everybody isn't doing it', *The Daily Telegraph*, 13 October 1994.

41 K.Wellings and J.Field *et al., Sexual Behaviour in Britain: the National Survey of Sexual Attitudes and Lifestyles*, Penguin, 1994.

42 Mrs Virginia Bottomley MP, quoted in James Le Fanu 'The high costs of the AIDS panic', *The Times*, 6 May 1993.

43 B.M.Craven, G.T.Stewart and M.Taghavi, *op. cit.*, p. 323.

44 Micheal Fumento, *op. cit.*, p. 384.

45 Michael Fumento, *op.cit.*, p. 384.

46 Susil Gupta, *op. cit.*

47 See Parliamentary debates House of Lords Hansard, Vol. 537, No.20, 11 June 1992.

48 Quoted in Stephen Green, *The Sexual Dead End*, Broadview, 1992, p. 56.

49 *Parents, Schools and Sex Education*, conducted by the National Foundation for Educational Research for the Health Education Authority, 1994.

50 Peter Weatherburn *et al., The Sexual Lifestyles of Gay and Bisexual Men in England and Wales Project*, Sigma, 1992, p. 34.

51 *AIDS & Sex Information for Young People*, AVERT, 1994.

52 *Disability: Information and Services* from the Equal Opportunities Unit, London Borough of Hounslow, 1992.

53 *Health Update 4: Sexual Health, op. cit.*, p. 33.

54 N.Ford and M.Inman, 'Safer sex in tourist resorts', *World Health Forum*, 1992, 13:1, 77-80.

55 Stephen J. Genuis and Shelagh K. Genuis, 'Adolescent sexual involvement: time for primary prevention', *The Lancet*, Vol. 345, 28 January 1995.

56 *Ibid*.

57 D.Hausser and P.A.Michaud, 'Does a condom promoting strategy (the Swiss STOP-AIDS campaign) modify sexual behaviour among adolescents?', *Paediatrics*, 1994, 93, 580-85.

6

Does Health Education Work?

James Le Fanu

Health education has great pretensions. The UK government's strategy for improving the health of the nation laid out in a document of that name published in July 1992 is based on the belief that health education can modify aspects of human behaviour – particularly dietary, smoking and sexual habits – which are implicated in problems as diverse as heart disease and strokes, teenage pregnancies and sexually transmitted diseases, accidents and suicides.[1]

It is therefore of considerable interest to know whether health education works and whether it is capable of preventing in some large measure these serious problems. Here one is immediately confronted by a paradox. Serious attempts to evaluate health education programmes have generally shown their results to be disappointing. On the other hand notable improvements in public health in recent years, such as the decline in coronary heart disease by almost 50% in the United States and the containment of a heterosexual AIDS epidemic, are frequently cited as evidence of the triumph of health education in persuading people to change their lives to their own benefit.

It is important to try and assess which of these two interpretations of the value of health education is correct, as they certainly cannot both be. If it is highly effective, one could argue that health education is so potent that it merits a marked increase in funding. If it is ineffective, the targets of Government policy are a mirage and the resources directed toward health education are being wasted.

The stated purpose of sex education

Before seeking to resolve this conflict of evidence, particularly in relation to sex education, it is worth pondering on the task that health education sets itself. Its purpose is "to obtain individual and voluntary health acts",[2] which makes it qualitatively different from the general purpose of education – to impart knowledge or intellectual skills. Thus, it is not enough simply to educate children about the mechanics of sex; they must also be persuaded, in the light of that knowledge, to behave in a way that will, for example, minimise the risk of teenage pregnancy or of acquiring a sexually transmitted disease.

This is unlikely to be easy, especially when, as is widely accepted, those who are most likely to benefit from health education messages are those least susceptible to them. Further, the nature of the behaviour which it is hoped to influence – as in the case of smoking, alcohol, food and sex – is pleasurable, not to say 'addictive', and is profoundly influenced by other cultural and societal norms which are difficult to counteract. The mere knowledge that certain practices might have untoward consequences is not necessarily sufficient incentive to avoid them. Everyone knows that smoking is harmful but such knowledge does not prevent up to a third of the adult population from lighting up.

The bridge between knowledge and action is *intention* and it is at this level that health education, if it is to work, must operate. Is it sufficiently potent to be able to influence the *intention* to stop smoking, switch to a healthy diet or behave in a sexually responsible manner? Merely articulating the question in this way is grounds for extreme scepticism about any claims to the effectiveness of health education.

Studies to date

What do the studies show that have sought to evaluate it? The most important evidence comes from two sources, a comprehensive review *Is Health Education Effective?* by Dr Alex Gatherer published by the Health Education Council (HEC)[3] and an analysis by Dr James Stout, 'Schools and Sex Education; Does it work?' from *Paediatrics*.[4]

First, the HEC review. Here Dr Gatherer points out: "the majority of the studies appear to be inadequately planned and their findings too vague and insufficiently controlled to be of much educational or practical value". Taking the 49 best studies examining the effects of mass media campaigns he finds that "short term changes of behaviour tended to disappear after a few months; if continued the long-term effect is no greater than a 10% change. Repeated campaigns may show a positive result for the first or second exposure, but little improvement or even a regression subsequently".

If better results are to be obtained, it seems necessary to combine mass media campaigns with much more intensive health education techniques as is shown by two heart disease prevention campaigns – the North Karelia project and Stamford seven county study. Both of these involved a concerted effort to supplement mass media campaigns with specialised training of health personnel, and the placing of information on healthy food in shops. In addition, a random section of the population were interviewed, examined and exhorted to change their life style. In the North Karelia study there was a highly significant reduction in risk-factor behaviour for coronary heart disease after five years and in the Stamford study an especially targeted high-risk group had changed their risky behaviour by almost 30% after two years. Essentially this means there had been major changes in smoking and exercise habit and a move towards what might be seen as a more healthy diet.

This sort of *Blitzkrieg* approach obviously can work but, as Dr John Farquhar who organised the Stamford study comments, the resources required are so enormous as to make this method of approach generally inapplicable.[5] Further, though both programmes achieved important changes in those aspects of lifestyle to which coronary heart disease is attributed, in neither was there a significant decline in actual heart disease mortality compared with controlled areas.

Turning to the analysis by Dr James Stout, the focus narrows to examine the specific question of whether sex education in schools has been shown to have a measurable influence on the incidence of teenage pregnancies. This is of particular interest because a reduction in pregnancy in this age group by health education is one of the targets set out in *The Health of the Nation*. Further, a report published by the RCOG in September 1991 argued that "improved" sex education by "better qualified" teachers was essential if the rising spiral of teenage abortion was to be controlled.[6]

What does Dr Stout find? The evidence of influence of health education on sexual activity is contradictory. Most studies show no effect, though one study found a somewhat lower figure of reported sexual activity in 15 and 16 year olds who had been subjected to a course in sex education compared to a control group who had not. Similarly sex education "appeared to have little effect on the use of effective birth control methods".

Finally, Dr Stout finds: "the results of the relevant studies are in almost uniform agreement that sex education programmes have no measurable effect on the incidence of teenage pregnancy". Dr Stout concludes that: "classroom sex education alone cannot be expected to change sexual behaviour in a direction that is opposite or in opposition to the sexual world as moulded by the television, film and advertising industries as well as peer group and adult role models".

Taken together then, these two reviews by Dr Gatherer of studies of health education in general and by Dr Stout on sex education, can only be interpreted as showing disappointing results.

Yet the belief that health education does work persists because of its supposed spectacular achievements in reducing the incidence of coronary heart disease over the last two decades by the promotion of a healthy diet[7] and in controlling the AIDS epidemic amongst homosexuals in Britain and preventing it from breaking out among the heterosexual population. Further, it is frequently argued that the sex education programmes in the Netherlands are responsible for that country having the lowest rate of teenage pregnancies in the western world.[8]

These two sources of evidence are irreconcilable. Health education cannot both be impotent as shown by the evaluative studies and at the same time spectacularly successful. It is thus important to try to determine whether the control of heart disease and AIDS are directly attributable to the effectiveness of health education or simply myths perpetuated by those in the business to keep themselves in work.

I have discussed in detail elsewhere the question of whether the promotion of a healthy diet through health education is responsible for the decline in coronary heart disease in the United States and other countries.[9] Suffice to say that there is absolutely no correlation between the changing pattern of coronary heart disease (CHD) and changes in total fat consumption. While heart disease has risen and fallen dramatically over the last 50 years, dietary patterns have remained essentially static. Certainly there have been small changes in the ratio of polyunsaturated to saturated fats in the national diet but these are essentially trivial and insufficient to influence substantially the risk of CHD.

The claim that health education can work because it has proved so efficacious in preventing CHD is clearly unfounded.

AIDS

Now I turn to AIDS – the subject of the health education campaign with the highest profile of all in recent years, funded between the years of 1986 and 1992 to the tune of a staggering £150 million. It is possible that the pattern of the AIDS epidemic in Britain, with a steady rise from small numbers in 1983 to a plateau in 1987/88 of just over 1,000 cases a year and a subsequent modest decline, can be attributed in part to these campaigns, but the evidence suggests the contrary.

It was apparent from the very earliest days of the AIDS epidemic, long before any substantial funds were allocated to health education, that knowledge of the seriousness of the disease and the possibility that it was transmitted by an infectious agent – even though the HIV virus had yet to be identified – produced a major change in sexual behaviour amongst homosexuals.

Thus, as early as September 1983, Dr Golubjatnikov of the University of Wisconsin writing in *The Lancet* reported a major fall amongst a cohort of homosexuals in the number of "sexual partners in the previous 30 days" over the preceding year. For example the numbers reporting "ten or more partners" had fallen from approximately 40% of those interviewed to fewer than 10%.[10]

There were similar changes in Britain, as can be shown by changes in incidence of diseases transmitted in the same way as AIDS, such as rectal gonorrhoea and hepatitis B. If one looks at the changing incidence of rectal gonorrhoea in male homosexuals in Leicester between 1982 and 1990, a major fall occurred from 1983/84 with only a small further decline from 1986-88 when no cases were recorded.[11]

From this it would seem that significant change in homosexual behaviour had already occurred – well before the launch of the high profile health education campaigns of 1986 onwards – and perhaps significantly, despite increasing funds allocated year on year, these campaigns failed to prevent an almost immediate relapse into unsafe sexual practices.

The main thrust of the AIDS campaigns has, however, been directed to preventing HIV transmission through casual heterosexual intercourse by promoting 'safe sex' and condom use in particular. It is conceivable that the heterosexual epidemic may have been prevented by this means, though this was never very likely in view of the very low levels of infection amongst heterosexuals who were not in an at-risk group (1.2% of the total).[12] In addition a study of sexual and contraceptive life styles of young people in 1992 found that 89% of respondents thought they had little or no chance of contracting HIV infection in the next few years, with most saying they did not feel the need to have bothered to use a condom.

In summary, homosexuals had adopted safe sex practices long before the health education campaigns started in 1986 and started relapsing back into unsafe practices from 1988 onwards. The campaign directed towards heterosexuals does not seemed to have convinced young people of the putative dangers of HIV transmission and it would thus seem unlikely that it prevented a heterosexual epidemic. All in all, this seems a rather poor return on an investment of £150 million.

Teenage pregnancy

Finally, it is necessary to examine critically the oft-repeated claim that the lower rates of teenage pregnancy in Sweden and the Netherlands compared to this country can be attributed to 'better' sex education.[13]

Certainly the teenage pregnancy rate in Britain (ages 15-19), at 45 per 1,000, is higher than both Sweden and the Netherlands with figures of 35 and 14 per 1,000 respectively.[14] The question whether this is related to sex education has been examined in a comparative study of nine industrialised nations.

Certainly sex education in Sweden is more comprehensive than in Britain. "Beginning at the age of seven the child is taught about physical differences, sexual anatomy, ovulation, conception, contraception and childbirth. These and many other topics of increasing complexity are covered during the entire period the individual is at school".[15]

However, the situation in the Netherlands is completely different. Here, "discussion of sex in the formal school programme is limited to the biological facts about reproduction . . . There is very little sex education in teacher training courses and many experienced teachers are reluctant to take on this sensitive subject".

There is a privately funded organisation prepared to offer sex education "which makes visits to classrooms upon invitations from the schools" but it would appear there is actually less formalised state sex education in the Netherlands than there is in Britain.

Taking together the experience of Britain, Sweden and the Netherlands it would thus appear that there is no clear relationship between the amount and quality of school sex education and the incidence of teenage pregnancies. It is thus necessary to invoke other factors – social, cultural and religious – to explain the differences. Once again we have found that the claims for the effectiveness of health education appear, when closely examined, to be without foundation.

Conclusion

At the beginning of this chapter, I identified the contradictory interpretations of the effectiveness of health education where scientific evaluative studies showed it to be essentially worthless, while substantial improvements in public health were attributed to it. I suggested they could not both be right.

Examining each of those claims of the benefit of health education in detail, the decline in coronary heart disease, the containment of the AIDS epidemic and the low incidence of teenage pregnancies in the Netherlands, we have found that the contribution of health education has been either marginal or irrelevant.

The answer to the question 'does health education work?' would seem to be 'very rarely'.

Notes

1 *The Health of the Nation*, Department of Health, 1992.

2 L.W.Green, *Health Education Monograph*, 1970, No. 30.

3 A.Gatherer *et al., Is Health Education Effective?*, Health Education Council, 1978.

4 Stout J.W. *et al., Paediatrics*, 1989, 83, 377.

5 J.W.Farquhar, *The Lancet*, 1977, 1, 119-122.

6 *Report of RCOG working party on unplanned pregnancy*, RCOG, 1991.

7 National Advisory Committee on Nutrition Education, report, London, 1983.

8 Massey, D.E., *British Journal of Family Planning*, 1992, 17, 97.

9 Le Fanu J. (Ed.), *Preventionitis: the Exaggerated Claims of Health Promotion,* Social Affairs Unit, 1994.

10 R. Golubjatnikov *et al., The Lancet*, 1983, 2, 681.

11 V.C.Riley, *The Lancet*, 1991, 337, 183.

12 CTR Report, 1993, 3, 77.

13 N.Ford, *British Journal of Family Planning*, 1993, 18, 119.

14 Jones E.F. *et al.*, *Family Planning Perspectives*, 1985, 17, 53.

15 Jones E.F. *et al.*, *Teenage Pregnancy in Industrialised Countries*, Yale University Press, 1986.

7

Teaching Sex in Schools: Does it Work?

Robert Whelan

The controversy

The introduction of sex education into the school curriculum has been a source of controversy for at least 30 years. Its advocates have claimed that young people need to be provided with accurate information about sexual relationships in order to allow them to make informed choices, and that being more knowledgeable will make them more responsible. Opponents argue that school-based sex education courses encourage promiscuity by conveying to young people the message that adults, and in particular those in authority over them like teachers, regard it as normal that they should be sexually active, even at young ages. By removing the stigma attached to early and promiscuous sexual activity, a powerful cultural mechanism for encouraging self-restraint is weakened.

Opponents further claim that sex education, particularly in the more explicit and prolonged courses, fills young people's heads with ideas which would not normally have occurred to them. Advocates argue that youngsters now live in a culture in which they are bombarded with sexual images and innuendo from every direction, and that, as the innocence of childhood scarcely exists any more, we need not worry about violating it.

Where is the proof?

One point on which both advocates and opponents agree is that sex education is intended to influence behaviour. Advocates argue that

88

it makes young people more responsible, opponents that it makes them more promiscuous. It should, therefore, be possible to test each hypothesis by examining the data relating to the problems which sex education was introduced to deal with, notably unwanted pregnancies and sexually transmitted diseases in young people.

On both counts, the period during which sex education has come to be accepted as part of the mission of educators has coincided with rapid, and indeed spectacular, rises in these two serious problems. If surveys are to be believed, teenage sexual activity has become extremely common now, compared with a generation ago. The British National Survey of Sexual Attitudes and Lifestyles found that the median age at first intercourse for females had fallen from 21 to 17 over a 40 year period, and from 20 to 17 for men.[1] However, we have no need to rely on surveys: the facts speak for themselves. In 1969, out of every 1,000 unmarried females aged 15-19, 52 became pregnant and seven of these had abortions. In 1991, 60 became pregnant and 22 had abortions. This is hardly a record of success.

The continuing spread of sexually transmitted diseases (STDs), especially among the young, is equally worrying. Between 1983 and 1993 the number of new cases seen at clinics increased from 547,437 to 661,261 – a rise of 21 per cent. This rise is almost entirely accounted for by new female cases. Furthermore, females between 16 and 19 have the highest rates of infection for gonorrhoea and chlamydia, and the second highest rate for herpes.[2]

However, even on this relatively solid statistical basis, there is no agreement between the two sides of the debate as to what conclusions we should draw. Opponents of sex education argue that it has clearly failed to solve the problems which it was specifically introduced to address. Advocates counter that sex education cannot be blamed for teenage sexual behaviour, as it is only one amongst many influences, and in any case it is not taught in all schools, nor in the same way in schools where it is taught. They further claim that sex education is having a salutary effect where it is taught properly, and that the figures would be worse without it.

The need for research

In the midst of such confusion, it would be reasonable to look to social scientists to evaluate the impact of sex education programmes. It is clearly true that young people today are subjected to a barrage of sexual information, much of it unhelpful, from advertising and the mass media. Sex education can never represent more than a fraction of their total intake of information on the subject. It is also true that sex education is a generic term which covers a wide variety of approaches, from chastity education to instruction in buggery and bestiality. We need to establish what sort of impact sex education makes on young people, and which approaches work best in achieving the development of that responsible attitude towards sexual behaviour which both sides in the debate claim to want. This should not be a particularly formidable task. It would involve the standard social science procedure of using control groups to compare those who have received sex education with those who have not in terms of their outcomes, particularly regarding unwanted pregnancies and STDs. It is perhaps surprising that few attempts have ever been made to do this.

No British research

There is a complete absence of British research of a serious nature and on a reasonable scale. Indeed, there appears to be a curious unwillingness amongst researchers to address the subject. The Health Education Authority, the government body charged with responsibility in this area, has never thought it worthwhile to carry out or sponsor research into the outcomes of the programmes it promotes. Instead it has entered the fray very much as a participant, publishing material of such a lewd and coarse nature that on two occasions ministers have had to intervene to suppress HEA publications.[3]

The National Survey of Sexual Attitudes and Lifestyles, sponsored by the Wellcome Foundation, was the most extensive survey of its type ever carried out in Britain. Nearly 19,000 people gave details of every imaginable aspect of their sex lives, including the nature of their sex education.[4] It was announced in advance that this would be correlated with age at first intercourse to see if those who had received sex education began their sex lives at a younger age. This would have made it the first British research on the subject based on a meaningful sample. However, when the report was published in early 1994 this information was not included. The official reason was shortage of time to analyse the data, but it would appear that these were the only answers out of dozens which were not written up for the final report.

In the absence of British data we are therefore reduced to looking at research which has been carried out in other countries, notably the USA, with all the disadvantages that implies in terms of trying to take into account the cultural differences between countries when considering the extent to which research carried out overseas is applicable here. Even on an international basis, however, there is a remarkable shortage of material. Indeed several academics who have looked at this question have commented on the surprising lack of hard research in a field which is so extremely controversial. A strongly critical review of the available research which was published in the *British Medical Journal* came to the conclusion that:

> Most sexual health interventions with young people are not evaluated. Of those that are, fewer than one in five meet the minimum criteria for methodologically sound evaluation . . . well designed studies are needed with a long enough follow-up to justify conclusions about the effectiveness of sexual health education in reaching . . . goals. In the absence of such evidence much of the present endeavour in sexual health promotion for young people can only be described as "knitting without a pattern".[5]

Ideological baggage

In such a minefield of values and beliefs, the consideration of the academic work which has been done is further complicated by the fact that much depends on the background and perspectives of those carrying it out. For example, in 1972 the Royal College of Obstetricians and Gynaecologists produced a report on teenage pregnancy which warned that: "Practically nothing is known about the effects of sex education programmes . . . (which may be) arousing curiosity and the desire to experiment. The rapidly rising incidence of unplanned pregnancies in the young age group gives some support to this idea".[6] In 1991 the RCOG published a further report on the same subject which made no such reservations, and which enthusiastically endorsed the provision of birth control and sex education to the young.[7] However, on this occasion only four of the report's 11 authors were fellows of the college, whilst others represented organisations actively and commercially involved with the provision of birth control and sex education. The report's conclusions, under the circumstances, were hardly surprising.

The Alan Guttmacher Institute study

In 1985 the journal *Family Planning Perspectives* published a study entitled 'Teenage Pregnancy in Developed Countries: Determinants and Policy Implications' which was hailed by sex education advocates as the 'proof' that explicit sex education and free provision of contraceptives would bring down teenage pregnancy rates. It is still highly regarded by the Sex Education Forum, an umbrella grouping of organisations including the Brook Advisory Centres, the Health Education Authority and the Catholic Marriage Advisory Council, which claims that:

> A large scale study of developed countries commissioned by the Guttmacher Institute and published in 1985, found that those countries with greater availability of sex education and birth control for young people have the lowest rates of teenage pregnancy, abortion and childrearing [*sic*].[8]

The first problem about the study is exactly the fact that it was commissioned by the Alan Guttmacher Institute, a wing of the Planned Parenthood Federation of America which is actively and lucratively involved in the provision of birth control and sex education. Research findings from the PPFA into the outcomes of such programmes must therefore be viewed in the same light as research into the connection between smoking and lung cancer carried out by tobacco companies.

92

However, that is not the only problem with the study. Its not-very-hidden agenda was to discredit the American way of life, and in particular the Reagan administration, which was felt to be unsympathetic to the birth control/population control lobby, by showing that teenage pregnancy rates were higher in the USA than in any other developed country.

The authors therefore attacked the American political and economic system, as well as the whole cultural and religious basis of American life, as contributory factors towards unwanted pregnancy, but reserved special animosity for the "powerful" and "well funded . . . constituencies that oppose contraception, sex education and legal abortion" in the USA.[9]

The basis of the attack was a survey of data on teenage pregnancies from 37 countries, from which five were chosen for detailed comparison with the USA. These were England and Wales, France, Canada, Sweden and the Netherlands. The selection of these countries was critical to the outcome of the study. As Robert Marshall and Charles Donovan pointed out:

. . . the AGI studied only those countries that had similar adolescent birth control programs and/or legal regimes and then contrasted the "results" with America. Ignored were countries like Japan, Ireland, Hong Kong, and Singapore, all of which have lower marital and nonmarital teen pregnancy rates and rely upon social pressures to discourage premature sexual experimentation. Also ignored were countries like Portugal, Spain, and individual states in the United States that, by law, policy, or tradition, restricted access to birth control and abortion and that have or had lower out-of-wedlock adolescent pregnancy rates than the United States as a whole.[10]

The idea that US teenagers were becoming pregnant owing to restrictions on their access to birth control and sex education becomes ludicrous when we consider that in the USA, which does not have socialised healthcare, birth control and abortion represent almost the only areas in which treatment is freely available, paid for by the government. Furthermore, in the field of sex education, programmes promoted by the PPFA and other lobby groups in the

USA have been so hair-raisingly explicit that they would not be permitted in the UK.

The World Health Organisation study

In fact, although the sex-education advocates pounced on this study, it contained very little on sex education owing to the absence of any meaningful body of data which could be used to show that some countries 'have sex education' while others do not. However, in 1993 it seemed that the debate over sex education had finally been resolved. Advocates around the world began citing a study produced for the World Health Organisation which was supposed to prove that sex education had no adverse effects, and that specifically it delayed sexual experimentation in pupils who had been exposed to it.

The basis of these claims was a piece of work produced for the WHO's 1993 AIDS conference in Berlin by Mariella Baldo, Peter Aggleton and Gary Slutkin, all of whom worked for the WHO's Global Programme on AIDS, which reviewed 19 studies of the effects of sex education and came to the conclusion that:

> Available evidence shows that *sex and AIDS education DO NOT promote earlier or increased sexual activity in young people. More positively, they may lead to an increased uptake of safer sex practices* [emphasis in original].

However this review of studies was not presented as a paper at the conference. Had this been the case it would have been published with the conference proceedings and made available for scrutiny. Extensive enquiries revealed that it had in fact been produced *as a poster*, pinned up in the conference hall. The fact that organisations like the Health Education Authority, the Family Planning Association, Catholic Aids Link, Family Health International and others had been relying on it to support their cause began to appear bizarre: it is not usual to cite posters in defence of one's position when debating a controversial topic.

In fact it makes no sense to discuss the Baldo poster without referring to the study on which it was based, entitled *Effects of Sex Education on Young People's Sexual Behaviour,* which had been carried out by Anne Grunseit and Susan Kippax of the National

Centre for HIV Social Research at Macquarie University in New South Wales, Australia. This had been commissioned by the Global Programme on AIDS of the World Health Organisation and delivered to them in 1993, prior to the Berlin AIDS conference.

It contained no original research but was rather a review of research findings from around the world. Grunseit and Kippax cited 35 studies[11], mostly from the USA but including some from western Europe (not the UK), Australia, Mexico and Thailand and succeeded in demonstrating, to their own satisfaction, that:

> . . . the overwhelming majority of articles reviewed here . . . find no support for the contention that sex education encourages sexual experimentation or increased activity. If any effect is observed . . . it is in the direction of postponed initiation of sexual intercourse and/or effective use of contraceptives (p.10).

They pinned their own colours to the mast in the preface which states that "sex education can have a beneficial effect on some of the potential outcomes of teenage sexual activity", but that "vocal and radical opponents, particularly in the United States, have severely limited its scope and implementation" (p.3). This is the same position as that adopted by the authors of the 1985 Alan Guttmacher Institute study.

Subsequent to the Berlin conference, Grunseit and Kippax pooled their resources with Baldo, Aggleton and Slutkin to produce an expanded version of the paper which is now circulating under the title of *Sex Education and Young People's Sexual Behaviour: A Review of Studies*. At the time of writing it has not been accepted for publication in an academic journal, nor has it been published by the WHO. This most frequently cited piece of research on the effects of sex education is thus still unavailable for study, unless interested parties can obtain copies of the typescript from the authors or from the WHO.

Sex Education and Young People's Sexual Behaviour draws on 46 different studies, 11 more than the first Grunseit/Kippax review, but the format and the conclusions are essentially the same.

The reader would certainly form the impression that there is a consensus, based on a large body of research, that sex education does no harm and may do good. The problems begin when we start to look at the studies which Grunseit *et al* are citing.[12] In several cases, there are over-simplifications or discrepancies between their accounts of the studies they purport to be reviewing and what those studies actually say. For example:

1. According to Grunseit *et al.*, a 1979 study from Australia[13] provided "no evidence that discussion of birth control increased the level of sexual experience". However, the only data collected was on children who had talked about birth control with their parents. According to the study, "sexual experience does not seem to be encouraged by parents talking to their children about birth control".[14] This is irrelevant to the controversy over sex education since no one is opposed to children acquiring information from their parents. The debate centres on the role of schools in this area.

2. According to Grunseit *et al.*, a study of the impact of sex education on college students in the USA[15] showed that "acquisition of knowledge of human sexuality did not result in increased participation in sexual intercourse". In fact, the study showed that male students who had taken the course increased their mean frequency of sexual intercourse from 42.1 times a year to 63.8 (an increase of 51 per cent). Males in the control group, who had not taken the course, reduced their mean frequency of intercourse over the same period from 63.1 to 47.7 times a year (a drop of 24 per cent). Amongst female students who took the course there was a drop in mean frequency of intercourse from 89.1 to 80.3 times a year (a drop of 10 per cent). Amongst female students in the control group, who had not taken the course, there was a drop from 63.9 to 59.8 times a year (a drop of 6 per cent). Females who had participated in the course increased their mean frequency of masturbation, while females in the control group decreased it. Furthermore, females who had participated in the course reported increased participation in oral sex.[16]

3. According to Grunseit *et al.*, a 1992 study[17] of 586 pupils in California who had been exposed to a sex education curriculum called *Reducing the Risk* showed that "data from the 18 month follow-up indicate that the program significantly delayed initiation of unprotected sex for those who were inexperienced prior to the program". This study is a six month follow up, not 18 months as stated, and comes to the conclusion that students exposed to *Reducing the Risk* "increased their frequency of birth control use but did not have a significantly lower rate of sexual activity or pregnancy. This finding puts this study in the company of numerous other pregnancy prevention projects that have not shown a significant reduction in pregnancies . . . The adolescents appear to have learned skills better than they used them".[18]

4. Grunseit *et al* refer to a 1991 study from the USA[19] which is, in fact, the 18 month follow-up referred to above, although they do not appear to realise this. The confusion arises because the 18 month follow-up was published before the six month follow-up, presumably because of delays in the peer-review process. Grunseit *et al.* interpret its findings as showing that, for those who were virgins at the start of the programme, there was a "significant delayed initiation of first intercourse at 18 months follow up [and] a significant reduction in proportion initiating unprotected sex after 18 months". However, the study is complicated and confusing. It states, on the one hand, that "among all . . . students who had not initiated intercourse prior to their exposure to the curriculum, the curriculum appears to have significantly reduced unprotected intercourse, either by delaying the onset of intercourse or by increasing the use of contraceptives"[20] and on the other hand that "the data indicate that the *RTR (Reducing the Risk)* curriculum did not affect the use of birth control at first intercourse or at most recent intercourse, nor did it affect the frequency of contraceptive use . . . it is puzzling that the curriculum did not significantly increase the practice of contraception among those students who initiated intercourse after program participation".[21]

The Kirby review

Douglas Kirby is the doyen of sex education researchers. For over a decade he has been monitoring research in the field, producing a series of overviews of which the most recent was commissioned by the US Centers for Disease Control in Atlanta. The brief given to Kirby and his team of researchers was to "review carefully the research on these programs [addressing problems associated with adolescent sexuality] and to assess their impact on behavior".[22]

Kirby and his team selected studies for inclusion in their review on the basis of three criteria. First, they had to be based on programmes carried out in schools. Second, the results must have been published in peer-reviewed journals. Third, the research must have measured reported sexual and contraceptive behaviour and its outcomes (*i.e.* pregnancy rates, birth rates or STD rates).

23 papers were found to meet the strict criteria, compared with 46 reviewed by Grunseit *et al.*, and only 16 were common to both studies. Some of the studies showed no impact at all of sex education on behaviour. Others showed desirable effects, such as postponing first intercourse. The important aspect of Kirby's work is that he has distinguished between the outcomes of different approaches to sex education in an attempt to isolate those factors most likely to make a programme successful.

Most importantly, he found that giving instruction on biological topics or contraception alone could lead to an earlier initiation of intercourse: the successful programmes combined information with "resistance skills" – teaching pupils to say no to sex. Comparing effective and ineffective programmes, he concludes that:

> Effective programs included a narrow focus on reducing sexual risk-taking behaviors that may lead to HIV-STD infection or to unintended pregnancy . . . effective programs focused upon a few specific behavioral goals, such as delaying the initiation of intercourse or using protection; relatively little time was spent addressing other sexuality issues, such as gender roles, dating and parenthood . . . the less effective curriculums tended to use a decision-making model in which the . . . students were implicitly instructed to make their own

decisions. This approach is in contrast to the methods used in the effective curriculums, which presented a clear stand and emphasized clear behavioral values and norms.[23]

An article by Stephen and Shelagh Genuis which appeared in *The Lancet* made the same important point. Concerned mainly with what they describe as "an unprecedented epidemic of sexually transmitted diseases, especially among adolescent and young adult women"[24], the authors criticise what they call "technological interventions" to deal with the problem by means of "better condoms, new female barrier methods, and vaccines against STD organisms", which are used as a means of dodging the more difficult issue of how to discourage early teenage sexual activity.

As an example of the uselessness of the "technological" approach they cite a Swiss study which showed that, over a three year period following the launch of a "safe sex" campaign to promote condom use:

. . . the percentage of 16-year-olds who had had sexual intercourse increased from 36 to 57% in girls, and from 58 to 63% in boys. The researchers suggested that previously many girls, without access to oral contraceptives, would not have engaged in sexual intercourse, and they commented: "obviously, purchasing a condom is easier than visiting a family planning center or gynecologist".[25]

As an example of the successful model, with the clearly stated goal of discouraging teenage sex, they cite an American programme targeted at high-risk 13-14 year olds which found that "by the end of the school year, young women who were not participants in the course were as much as 15 times more likely to have begun sex than were participants".[26]

In spite of these lessons from other countries, it is sad to have to report that almost all of the material produced by the largest sex education lobby groups in the UK, such as the Family Planning Association and the Brook Advisory Centres, conforms to the model of the ineffective curriculums, as defined by Kirby and Genuis. The idea that there are any moral or behavioural norms is shunned, and indeed most of the effort goes into convincing pupils that any decisions they make about sex are of equal value, that there are no rights and wrongs, and that everything is a matter of opinion. The idea that sex education should discourage children from becoming sexually active would be regarded as ridiculous by most of the leading lights in the field.

Sex education and pregnancy prevention

Although Kirby probably knows more about the state of sex education research than anyone, and although personally committed to sex education, even he has to admit that there is little evidence to show that sex education can reduce the rate of teen pregnancy, which most people would regard as its most important role:

> It remains unclear whether school-based or school-linked reproductive health services, either by themselves or in addition to education programs, significantly decrease pregnancy or birth rates . . . There are serious limitations in the research on pregnancy prevention programs, and little is known with much certainty.[27]

The most devastating attack on the whole edifice of sex education to be published in the mainstream media came from Barbara Dafoe Whitehead in the October 1994 edition of the American magazine *Atlantic Monthly*.[28] She began by outlining the arguments for and against sex education, then suggested that, at some time, the sex educators had to face up to what she called "the reality test": after all the theorizing, it should be possible to show if it works or not.

She focused her attentions on the state of New Jersey, which is a sort of showcase for what the sex education advocates regard as good practice. Comprehensive sex education became mandatory in 1980; the state was the first to require it for primary schools; and its efforts "have earned New Jersey the equivalent of a five star rating from the Sex Information and Education Council of the US (SIECUS)".[29] In spite of this:

> If sex education has had a significant impact on teenage sexual behavior in New Jersey, there is little evidence to show it. The advocates cannot point to any evaluative studies of

comprehensive sex education in the state. Absent such specific measures, one can only fall back on gross measures like the glum statistics on unwed teenage childbearing in the state. In 1980, 67.6 per cent of teenage births were to unmarried mothers; eleven years later the figure had increased to 84 per cent . . . it is hard for advocates to claim that the state with the nation's fourth highest percentage of unwed teenage births is a showcase for their approach.[30]

Nevertheless, as Whitehead points out, the advocates are not dismayed by the lack of any academic research base for their policies because:

sex education is a policy crafted outside the precincts of the academy . . . The unifying core of comprehensive sex education is not intellectual but ideological. Its mission is to defend and extend the freedoms of the sexual revolution[31] . . . the sex education leaders are not researchers or policy analysts or child-development experts but public sector entrepreneurs: advocates, independent consultants, family planners, freelance curriculum writers, speciality publishers and diversity educators . . . their principal task is not to serve the public but to promote their ideology.[32]

Advocates of sex education often claim that opinion polls show that a majority of parents wish their children to be sex educated at school. This raises the question of how much parents actually know about what is being taught and what are the intentions of the teachers. Of course parents want their children to learn to be responsible in their sexual behaviour, and able to make informed decisions. That does not mean that they wish them to be turned into cannon fodder in the sexual revolution. As the teenage casualties of the permissive society mount, perhaps it is time to ask ourselves if we really want our children to be caught in the crossfire of opposing ideologies. In the absence of any firm evidence that sex education programmes are reducing teenage pregnancies and STDs, perhaps we should even consider calling a ceasefire.

The author is grateful to Paul Atkin, Dr John Guly and Eric Lee for their help with the research for this chapter.

101

Notes

1 Johnson, A.M., Wadsworth, J., Wellings, K., Field, J., *Sexual Attitudes and Lifestyles*, Oxford: Blackwell Scientific Publications, 1994, pp. 70-71.

2 *Summary of information from form KC60: New cases seen at NHS genito-urinary medicine clinics in England,* published by the Department of Health, London, 1993 Annual Figures.

3 In 1988 10,000 copies of the HEA's teaching pack *Teaching about HIV and AIDS* were shredded after ministers objected to the inclusion of contact lists of homosexual organisations and agencies. In 1994 distribution of the HEA's booklet *Your Pocket Guide to Sex* was stopped by the Health Minister Brian Mawhinney who found it "distasteful and smutty" (*Sunday Telegraph,* 27 March 1994).

4 Johnson, A.M. *et al., op.cit.* The questions on sex education were numbers 17 and 18 in the Survey Questionnaire, reproduced on pp.396-7.

5 Oakley, A., *et al.,* "Sexual health education interventions for young people: a methodological review", *British Medical Journal,* Vol. 310, 21 January 1995, p. 161.

6 *Unplanned Pregnancy,* Royal College of Obstetricians and Gynaecologists, 1972.

7 *Report of the RCOG Working Party on Unplanned Pregnancy,* Royal College of Obstetricians and Gynaecologists, 1991.

8 Sex Education Forum leaflet, *A Framework for School Sex Education,* London: National Children's Bureau, undated.

9 Jones, E.F. *et al.,* "Teenage Pregnancy in Developed Countries: Determinants and Policy Implications", *Family Planning Perspectives,* Vol. 17, No. 2, March/April 1985, p. 60.

10 Marshall, R. and Donovan, C., *Blessed Are the Barren: The Social Policy of Planned Parenthood,* San Francisco: Ignatius Press, 1991, p. 90.

11 The poster by Baldo *et al.* listed 19 of these 35 studies. Amongst those omitted was a 1986 study from the USA which found that "adolescent women who have previously taken a sex education course are somewhat more likely than those who have not to initiate sexual activity at ages 15 and 16". See Marsiglio, W. and Mott, F., "The impact of sex education on sexual activity, contraceptive use and pre-marital pregnancy among American teenagers", *Family Planning Perspectives*, Vol.18, No.4, p. 151, 1986.

12 One over-simplification which occurred in the original Grunseit/Kippax paper was apparently picked up and changed in the revision of the material to incorporate the work of Baldo *et al.* A 1992 study of AIDS education had been described as showing that "AIDS and sex education were associated with decreased levels of sex partners and intercourse frequency and increased levels of condom use". In fact the study reported that "Having been taught resistance skills was associated with significant reductions both in the number of sexual partners in the last year and in the frequency of intercourse . . . instructions in the skills needed to resist sexual intercourse had a stronger independent influence on reducing sexual activity than did instruction about AIDS or birth control". (See: Ku, L.C., Sonenstein, F.L., Pleck, J.H., "The Association of AIDS Education and Sex Education with Sexual Behavior and Condom Use Among Teenage Men", *Family Planning Perspectives*, 1992, Vol. 24, No. 3, pp. 103 and 104.) The study was described in different terms in the enlarged and revised version of the paper.

13 Siedlecky, S., *Sex and Contraception Before Marriage: A Study of Attitudes and Experience of Never Married Youth in Melbourne, Australia*, Australian Family Formation Project Monograph No. 7, Department of Demography, Institute of Advanced Studies, The Australian National University, Canberra, 1979.

14 *Ibid.*, p. 65.

15 Davidson Sr, J.K, Darling, C.A., "The Impact of College-Level Sex Education on Sexual Knowledge, Attitudes and Practices: The Knowledge/Sexual Experimentation Myth Revisited", *Deviant Behavior*, Vol. 7, 1986, pp. 13-30.

16 *Ibid.*, pp. 25-26.

17 Barth, R.P., Fetro, J.V., Leland, N., Volkan, K., "Preventing Adolescent Pregnancy with Social and Cognitive Skills", *Journal of Adolescent Research*, Vol. 7 No. 2, April 1992, pp. 208-232.

18 *Ibid.*, pp. 228 and 229.

19 Kirby, D., Barth, R.P., Leland, N., Fetro, J.V., "Reducing the Risk: Impact of a New Curriculum on Sexual Risk-Taking", *Family Planning Perspectives*, Vol. 23, No. 6, 1991, pp. 253-263.

20 *Ibid.*, p. 253.

21 *Ibid.*, p. 261.

22 Kirby, D. *et al.*, "School-Based Programs to Reduce Sexual Risk Behaviors: A Review of Effectiveness", *Public Health Reports*, Vol. 109, No. 3, 1994, p. 339.

23 *Ibid.*, pp. 353 and 355.

24 Genuis, S.G., Genuis, S.K., "Adolescent sexual involvement: time for primary prevention", *The Lancet*, Vol. 345, Jan. 28 1995, pp. 240-241.

25 Hausser, D., Michaud, P.A., "Does a condom-promoting strategy (the Swiss STOP-AIDS campaign) modify sexual behavior among adolescents?", *Pediatrics*, Vol. 93, 1994, pp. 580-85.

26 Howard, M., McCabe, J.B., "Helping teenagers postpone sexual involvement", *Family Planning Perspectives*, Vol. 22, 1990, pp. 21-26.

27 Kirby, D. *et al.*, *op. cit*, pp. 357 and 358.

28 Whitehead, B.D., "The Failure of Sex Education", *The Atlantic Monthly*, October 1994, pp. 55-80.

29 *Ibid.*, p. 56.

30 *Ibid.*, p. 70.

31 Support for Whitehead's view was provided by Alan Guttmacher himself when he announced that "The answer to winning the battle for elective abortion once and for all is sex education" (*Washington Star*, 3 May 1973).

32 *Ibid.*, p. 70.

Appendix

Local Action for Parents

If the unsatisfactory situation should arise where the instruction to be given is against the parents' deeply held religious or philosophical beliefs, here is the correct procedure:

1. Seek an appointment with the Head Teacher. Take your wife, husband, or another parent with you. If you have not been informed or consulted before sex education was embarked upon, ask why not, and quote the Education Acts (1944, 1980, 1986 and 1993). Ask for a written copy of the syllabus.

2. Ask about the context in which information on sexual intercourse and childbirth is given. Note the answers carefully.

3. Ask to see all the sex education material: books, leaflets, packs, slides and videos which are used in the school. Note the titles and publishers of any material about which you are concerned.

4. Ask whether any particular organisations are involved in sex education in the school. Some organisations are associated with the sale of contraceptives, the provision of abortions and the promotion of homosexual activity.

5. If you are not satisfied tell the Head Teacher this and why. State your beliefs and cultural norms – you do not have to justify them. Do not be drawn into heated arguments. Ask what steps will be taken to see that your child is not indoctrinated with any other standards and values.

6. Write an account of what has happened and send a copy to the Head Teacher asking him or her to confirm your understanding of the school's policy and the ways in which your wishes will be met including, if necessary, your right to withdraw your child from offensive information.

7. If you are not satisfied with the response of the Head Teacher, ask for an appointment with the Chairman and Parent Governors of the school.

8. The last word locally on publicly provided education is that of the Director of Education for your area.

9. If you do not gain satisfaction from the Director of Education and the matter is still not resolved there is the right of appeal to the Secretary of State for Education. For further information on this procedure refer to chapter 3, 'The Law on Sex Education', by Colin Hart.

10. If you feel strongly about the situation, public exposure may be the only effective way of ensuring that your voice is heard. Bring your concern to the attention of your local papers, radio and TV.

Do not be afraid to act decisively as defenders of your child's well-being. You have been given legal rights. Why not use them?

Biographical Notes

Dr Melvin Anchell is a neuropsychiatrist and a Fellow of the American Society of Psychoanalytic Physicians. He has had a private practice in General Medicine and Psychiatry since 1948, and has been an active member of numerous American medical associations. His books include *Sex and Insanity*; he wrote the *Effects Report* critique for President Johnson's Commission on Obscenity. He is frequently called on to be an expert witness in pornography and obscenity cases at Federal and State levels.

Paul Atkin is a graduate of the University of Sunderland where he read Politics and Religion and was awarded the John Lilburne prize for politics. He took a postgraduate diploma in personnel management at Heriot Watt University in Edinburgh, is a graduate member of the Institute of Personnel and Development and works in personnel management. A pro-life activist with special interest in sex education, abortion, bio-ethics, euthanasia and the family, he has appeared on radio and TV and written articles on these subjects in specialist magazines.

Paul Danon is a graduate in English who has worked in advertising, journalism and technical writing. Now a public relations consultant and freelance editor, he is also secretary to the Catholic Writers' Guild and a school governor. He is married with four school-age children.

Diana Elles has had a distinguished career as a lawyer and in public office and was raised to the peerage as Baroness Elles of the City of Westminster in 1972. She was Vice-President of the European Parliament from 1982-87 and Chairman of the Legal Affairs and Citizens Rights Committee of the European Parliament from 1987-89. A former member of the United Nations Sub-Commission for Prevention of Discrimination and Protection of Minorities, she was a member of the House of Lords European Community Select Committee from 1984 to 1994.

Colin Hart is Director of the Christian Institute, based in Newcastle upon Tyne and secretary of CATS, the Christian parent teacher association. Formerly a teacher in a comprehensive school, he has a particular interest in the relationship between religious education and the law and has had papers published in *The Law and Education* and *Christian Law Review*.

Dr James Le Fanu, a graduate of Cambridge University, is a general practitioner in London and also medical columnist of the *Sunday Telegraph* and a weekly contributor to *The Times* and the *Daily Telegraph*. He is author of *Eat your Heart Out, Healthwise: An intelligent guide for the Over 60s, A Phantom Carnage: the myth that low income kills* and *Chattering International: how Unicef fails the world's poorest children*. He has also contributed numerous articles to edited books and journals.

Patricia Morgan is a sociologist who has specialised in criminology. She held the Morris Finer research scholarship at the London School of Economics. She is the author of a number of books including *Delinquent Fantasies* on juvenile crime and the juvenile justice system, as well as contributing to *Criminal Welfare on Trial*. She has recently written *Facing Up to Family Income*, on government policy and the economic status of the family today; and *The Hidden Costs of Childcare*, on the harmful effects of childcare on many aspects of child development. She is a frequent contributor to various newspaper and magazines, as well as radio and TV programmes, on matters of crime and family policy. Dr Morgan is married and has two young children.

Valerie Riches trained as a social worker. She is Director of the Family Education Trust and Family & Youth Concern and regularly expresses the viewpoint of these organisations in the national press and on radio and televison. She has lectured in all five continents and is the author of several publications including *Sex and Social Engineering* and *Who Cares for Children?* Mrs Riches is married with two children.

Robert Whelan read English at Trinity College, Cambridge, and is now Assistant Director of the Health and Welfare Unit of the Institute of Economic Affairs. He has written and produced a series of educational videos for the Family Education Trust, including *Facing Facts on Population, The Great Population Hoax, The Truth about AIDS* and *The Three Rs of Family Life*. He has lectured and broadcast widely on population issues, and is the author of *Mounting Greenery* (published by the IEA Education Unit) and *Choices in Childbearing* (published by the Committee on Population and the Economy).